# LION'S HONEY

Also by David Grossman

*Death As a Way of Life: Dispatches from Jerusalem* (2003)

*The Body* (untranslated, 2002)

*Someone to Run With* (2000)

*Be My Knife* (1998)

*The Zigzag Kid* (1994)

*Sleeping on a Wire: Conversations with Israeli Palestinians* (1992)

*The Book of Intimate Grammar* (1991)

*The Yellow Wind* (1987)

*See Under: Love* (1986)

*The Smile of the Lamb* (1983)

*Duel* (1982)

Myths are universal and timeless stories that reflect and shape our lives – they explore our desires, our fears, our longings, and provide narratives that remind us what it means to be human. *The Myths* series brings together some of the world's finest writers, each of whom has retold a myth in a contemporary and memorable way. Other authors in the series include: Chinua Achebe, Margaret Atwood, Karen Armstrong, A.S. Byatt, Milton Hatoum, Natsuo Kirino, Alexander McCall Smith, Victor Pelevin, Ali Smith, Donna Tartt, Su Tong and Jeanette Winterson.

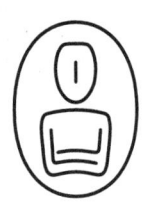

# LION'S HONEY

*The Myth of Samson*

David Grossman

Translated from the Hebrew by Stuart Schoffman

Alfred A. Knopf Canada

PUBLISHED BY ALFRED A. KNOPF CANADA

Copyright © 2005 David Grossman
Translation copyright © 2006 Stuart Schoffman
Published by arrangement with Canongate Books Ltd., Edinburgh, Scotland

Knopf Canada and colophon are trademarks.
www.randomhouse.ca


Library and Archives Canada Cataloguing in Publication
Grossman, David
    Lion's honey : the myth of Samson / David Grossman.

(The myths series)

ISBN-13: 978-0-676-97421-8
ISBN-10: 0-676-97421-X

1. Samson (Biblical judge).  I. Title.  II. Series: Myths series.

PJ5054.G738L55 2006       222'.32       C2006-901557-0


Designed by Pentagram
Typeset in Van Dijck MT Regular by Palimpsest Book Production Ltd,
Polmont, Stirlingshire

First Edition
Printed and bound in the United States of America

10 9 8 7 6 5 4 3 2 1

# The Book of Judges

## Chapters 13–16

*from* The Authorised King James Version

# Chapter 13

And the children of Israel did evil again in the sight of the LORD; and the LORD delivered them into the hand of the Philistines forty years.

2 ¶ And there was a certain man of Zorah, of the family of the Danites, whose name *was* Manoah; and his wife *was* barren, and bare not.

3 And the angel of the LORD appeared unto the woman, and said unto her, Behold now, thou *art* barren, and bearest not: but thou shalt conceive, and bear a son.

4 Now therefore beware, I pray thee, and drink not wine nor strong drink, and eat not any unclean *thing:*

5 For, lo, thou shalt conceive, and bear a son; and no razor shall come on his head: for the child shall be a Nazarite unto God from the womb: and he shall begin to deliver Israel out of the hand of the Philistines.

6 ¶ Then the woman came and told her

husband, saying, A man of God came unto me, and his countenance *was* like the countenance of an angel of God, very terrible: but I asked him not whence he *was*, neither told he me his name:

7 But he said unto me, Behold, thou shalt conceive, and bear a son; and now drink no wine nor strong drink, neither eat any unclean *thing:* for the child shall be a Nazarite to God from the womb to the day of his death.

8 ¶ Then Manoah intreated the LORD, and said, O my Lord, let the man of God which thou didst send come again unto us, and teach us what we shall do unto the child that shall be born.

9 And God hearkened to the voice of Manoah; and the angel of God came again unto the woman as she sat in the field: but Manoah her husband *was* not with her.

10 And the woman made haste, and ran, and shewed her husband, and said unto him, Behold, the man hath appeared unto me, that came unto me the *other* day.

11 And Manoah arose, and went after his wife, and came to the man, and said unto him, *Art* thou

the man that spakest unto the woman? And he said, I *am*.

12 And Manoah said, Now let thy words come to pass. How shall we order the child, and *how* shall we do unto him?

13 And the angel of the LORD said unto Manoah, Of all that I said unto the woman let her beware.

14 She may not eat of any *thing* that cometh of the vine, neither let her drink wine or strong drink, nor eat any unclean *thing:* all that I commanded her let her observe.

15 ¶ And Manoah said unto the angel of the LORD, I pray thee, let us detain thee, until we shall have made ready a kid for thee.

16 And the angel of the LORD said unto Manoah, Though thou detain me, I will not eat of thy bread: and if thou wilt offer a burnt offering, thou must offer it unto the LORD. For Manoah knew not that he *was* an angel of the LORD.

17 And Manoah said unto the angel of the LORD, What *is* thy name, that when thy sayings come to pass we may do thee honour?

18 And the angel of the L<small>ORD</small> said unto him, Why askest thou thus after my name, seeing it *is* secret?

19 So Manoah took a kid with a meat offering, and offered *it* upon a rock unto the L<small>ORD</small>: and *the angel* did wondrously; and Manoah and his wife looked on.

20 For it came to pass, when the flame went up toward heaven from off the altar, that the angel of the L<small>ORD</small> ascended in the flame of the altar. And Manoah and his wife looked on *it*, and fell on their faces to the ground.

21 But the angel of the L<small>ORD</small> did no more appear to Manoah and to his wife. Then Manoah knew that he *was* an angel of the L<small>ORD</small>.

22 And Manoah said unto his wife, We shall surely die, because we have seen God.

23 But his wife said unto him, If the L<small>ORD</small> were pleased to kill us, he would not have received a burnt offering and a meat offering at our hands, neither would he have shewed us all these *things*, nor would as at this time have told us *such things* as these.

24 ¶ And the woman bare a son, and called his name Samson: and the child grew, and the LORD blessed him.

25 And the Spirit of the LORD began to move him at times in the camp of Dan between Zorah and Eshtaol.

# Chapter 14

And Samson went down to Timnath, and saw a woman in Timnath of the daughters of the Philistines.

2 And he came up, and told his father and his mother, and said, I have seen a woman in Timnath of the daughters of the Philistines: now therefore get her for me to wife.

3 Then his father and his mother said unto him, *Is there* never a woman among the daughters of thy brethren, or among all my people, that thou goest to take a wife of the uncircumcised Philistines? And Samson said unto his father, Get her for me; for she pleaseth me well.

4 But his father and his mother knew not that it *was* of the LORD, that he sought an occasion against the Philistines: for at that time the Philistines had dominion over Israel.

5 ¶ Then went Samson down, and his father and his mother, to Timnath, and came to the vineyards

of Timnath: and, behold, a young lion roared against him.

6 And the Spirit of the LORD came mightily upon him, and he rent him as he would have rent a kid, and *he had* nothing in his hand: but he told not his father or his mother what he had done.

7 And he went down, and talked with the woman; and she pleased Samson well.

8 ¶ And after a time he returned to take her, and he turned aside to see the carcase of the lion: and, behold, *there was* a swarm of bees and honey in the carcase of the lion.

9 And he took thereof in his hands, and went on eating, and came to his father and mother, and he gave them, and they did eat: but he told not them that he had taken the honey out of the carcase of the lion.

10 ¶ So his father went down unto the woman: and Samson made there a feast; for so used the young men to do.

11 And it came to pass, when they saw him, that they brought thirty companions to be with him.

12 ¶ And Samson said unto them, I will now put forth a riddle unto you: if ye can certainly declare it me within the seven days of the feast, and find *it* out, then I will give you thirty sheets and thirty change of garments:

13 But if ye cannot declare *it* me, then shall ye give me thirty sheets and thirty change of garments. And they said unto him, Put forth thy riddle, that we may hear it.

14 And he said unto them, Out of the eater came forth meat, and out of the strong came forth sweetness. And they could not in three days expound the riddle.

15 And it came to pass on the seventh day, that they said unto Samson's wife, Entice thy husband, that he may declare unto us the riddle, lest we burn thee and thy father's house with fire: have ye called us to take that we have? *is it* not *so?*

16 And Samson's wife wept before him, and said, Thou dost but hate me, and lovest me not: thou hast put forth a riddle unto the children of my people, and hast not told *it* me. And he said

unto her, Behold, I have not told *it* my father nor my mother, and shall I tell *it* thee?

17 And she wept before him the seven days, while their feast lasted: and it came to pass on the seventh day, that he told her, because she lay sore upon him: and she told the riddle to the children of her people.

18 And the men of the city said unto him on the seventh day before the sun went down, What *is* sweeter than honey? and what *is* stronger than a lion? And he said unto them, If ye had not plowed with my heifer, ye had not found out my riddle.

19 ¶ And the Spirit of the LORD came upon him, and he went down to Ashkelon, and slew thirty men of them, and took their spoil, and gave change of garments unto them which expounded the riddle. And his anger was kindled, and he went up to his father's house.

20 But Samson's wife was *given* to his companion, whom he had used as his friend.

# Chapter 15

But it came to pass within a while after, in the time of wheat harvest, that Samson visited his wife with a kid; and he said, I will go in to my wife into the chamber. But her father would not suffer him to go in.

2 And her father said, I verily thought that thou hadst utterly hated her; therefore I gave her to thy companion: *is* not her younger sister fairer than she? take her, I pray thee, instead of her.

3 ¶ And Samson said concerning them, Now shall I be more blameless than the Philistines, though I do them a displeasure.

4 And Samson went and caught three hundred foxes, and took firebrands, and turned tail to tail, and put a firebrand in the midst between two tails.

5 And when he had set the brands on fire, he let *them* go into the standing corn of the Philistines, and burnt up both the shocks, and also the standing corn, with the vineyards *and* olives.

6 ¶ Then the Philistines said, Who hath done this? And they answered, Samson, the son in law of the Timnite, because he had taken his wife, and given her to his companion. And the Philistines came up, and burnt her and her father with fire.

7 ¶ And Samson said unto them, Though ye have done this, yet will I be avenged of you, and after that I will cease.

8 And he smote them hip and thigh with a great slaughter: and he went down and dwelt in the top of the rock Etam.

9 ¶ Then the Philistines went up, and pitched in Judah, and spread themselves in Lehi.

10 And the men of Judah said, Why are ye come up against us? And they answered, To bind Samson are we come up, to do to him as he hath done to us.

11 Then three thousand men of Judah went to the top of the rock Etam, and said to Samson, Knowest thou not that the Philistines *are* rulers over us? what *is* this *that* thou hast done unto us? And he said unto them, As they did unto me, so have I done unto them.

12 And they said unto him, We are come down to bind thee, that we may deliver thee into the hand of the Philistines. And Samson said unto them, Swear unto me, that ye will not fall upon me yourselves.

13 And they spake unto him, saying, No; but we will bind thee fast, and deliver thee into their hand: but surely we will not kill thee. And they bound him with two new cords, and brought him up from the rock.

14 ¶ *And* when he came unto Lehi, the Philistines shouted against him: and the Spirit of the LORD came mightily upon him, and the cords that *were* upon his arms became as flax that was burnt with fire, and his bands loosed from off his hands.

15 And he found a new jawbone of an ass, and put forth his hand, and took it, and slew a thousand men therewith.

16 And Samson said, With the jawbone of an ass, heaps upon heaps, with the jaw of an ass have I slain a thousand men.

17 And it came to pass, when he had made an

end of speaking, that he cast away the jawbone out of his hand, and called that place Ramath-lehi.

18 ¶ And he was sore athirst, and called on the LORD, and said, Thou hast given this great deliverance into the hand of thy servant: and now shall I die for thirst, and fall into the hand of the uncircumcised?

19 But God clave an hollow place that *was* in the jaw, and there came water thereout; and when he had drunk, his spirit came again, and he revived: wherefore he called the name thereof En-hak-kore, which *is* in Lehi unto this day.

20 And he judged Israel in the days of the Philistines twenty years.

# Chapter 16

Then went Samson to Gaza, and saw there an harlot, and went in unto her.

2 *And it was told* the Gazites, saying, Samson is come hither. And they compassed *him* in, and laid wait for him all night in the gate of the city, and were quiet all the night, saying, In the morning, when it is day, we shall kill him.

3 And Samson lay till midnight, and arose at midnight, and took the doors of the gate of the city, and the two posts, and went away with them, bar and all, and put *them* upon his shoulders, and carried them up to the top of an hill that *is* before Hebron.

4 ¶ And it came to pass afterward, that he loved a woman in the valley of Sorek, whose name *was* Delilah.

5 And the lords of the Philistines came up unto her, and said unto her, Entice him, and see wherein his great strength *lieth*, and by what *means* we may

prevail against him, that we may bind him to afflict him: and we will give thee every one of us eleven hundred *pieces* of silver.

6 ¶ And Delilah said to Samson, Tell me, I pray thee, wherein thy great strength *lieth*, and wherewith thou mightest be bound to afflict ·thee.

7 And Samson said unto her, If they bind me with seven green withs that were never dried, then shall I be weak, and be as another man.

8 Then the lords of the Philistines brought up to her seven green withs which had not been dried, and she bound him with them.

9 Now *there were* men lying in wait, abiding with her in the chamber. And she said unto him, The Philistines *be* upon thee, Samson. And he brake the withs, as a thread of tow is broken when it toucheth the fire. So his strength was not known.

10 And Delilah said unto Samson, Behold, thou hast mocked me, and told me lies: now tell me, I pray thee, wherewith thou mightest be bound.

11 And he said unto her, If they bind me fast with new ropes that never were occupied, then shall I be weak, and be as another man.

12 Delilah therefore took new ropes, and bound him therewith, and said unto him, The Philistines *be* upon thee, Samson. And *there were* liers in wait abiding in the chamber. And he brake them from off his arms like a thread.

13 And Delilah said unto Samson, Hitherto thou hast mocked me, and told me lies: tell me wherewith thou mightest be bound. And he said unto her, If thou weavest the seven locks of my head with the web.

14 And she fastened *it* with the pin, and said unto him, The Philistines *be* upon thee, Samson. And he awaked out of his sleep, and went away with the pin of the beam, and with the web.

15 ¶ And she said unto him, How canst thou say, I love thee, when thine heart *is* not with me? thou hast mocked me these three times, and hast not told me wherein thy great strength *lieth*.

16 And it came to pass, when she pressed him daily with her words, and urged him, *so* that his soul was vexed unto death;

17 That he told her all his heart, and said unto her, There hath not come a razor upon mine head;

for I *have been* a Nazarite unto God from my mother's womb: if I be shaven, then my strength will go from me, and I shall become weak, and be like any *other* man.

18 And when Delilah saw that he had told her all his heart, she sent and called for the lords of the Philistines, saying, Come up this once, for he hath shewed me all his heart. Then the lords of the Philistines came up unto her, and brought money in their hand.

19 And she made him sleep upon her knees; and she called for a man, and she caused him to shave off the seven locks of his head; and she began to afflict him, and his strength went from him.

20 And she said, The Philistines *be* upon thee, Samson. And he awoke out of his sleep, and said, I will go out as at other times before, and shake myself. And he wist not that the LORD was departed from him.

21 ¶ But the Philistines took him, and put out his eyes, and brought him down to Gaza, and bound him with fetters of brass; and he did grind in the prison house.

22 Howbeit the hair of his head began to grow again after he was shaven.

23 Then the lords of the Philistines gathered them together for to offer a great sacrifice unto Dagon their god, and to rejoice: for they said, Our god hath delivered Samson our enemy into our hand.

24 And when the people saw him, they praised their god: for they said, Our god hath delivered into our hands our enemy, and the destroyer of our country, which slew many of us.

25 And it came to pass, when their hearts were merry, that they said, Call for Samson, that he may make us sport. And they called for Samson out of the prison house; and he made them sport: and they set him between the pillars.

26 And Samson said unto the lad that held him by the hand, Suffer me that I may feel the pillars whereupon the house standeth, that I may lean upon them.

27 Now the house was full of men and women; and all the lords of the Philistines *were* there; and *there were* upon the roof about three thousand men

and women, that beheld while Samson made sport.

28 And Samson called unto the LORD, and said, O Lord GOD, remember me, I pray thee, and strengthen me, I pray thee, only this once, O God, that I may be at once avenged of the Philistines for my two eyes.

29 And Samson took hold of the two middle pillars upon which the house stood, and on which it was borne up, of the one with his right hand, and of the other with his left.

30 And Samson said, Let me die with the Philistines. And he bowed himself with *all his* might; and the house fell upon the lords, and upon all the people that *were* therein. So the dead which he slew at his death were more than *they* which he slew in his life.

31 Then his brethren and all the house of his father came down, and took him, and brought *him* up, and buried him between Zorah and Eshtaol in the buryingplace of Manoah his father. And he judged Israel twenty years.

# Foreword

'Samson the hero' is what every Jewish child, the first time he or she hears the story, learns to call him. And that, more or less, is how he has been represented over the years, in hundreds of works of art, theatre and film, in the literatures of many languages: a mythic hero and fierce warrior, the man who tore apart a lion with his bare hands, the charismatic leader of the Jews in their wars against the Philistines, and, without a doubt, one of the most tempestuous and colourful characters in the Hebrew Bible.

But the way that I read the story in the pages of my bible – the Book of Judges, chapters 13 to 16 – runs against the grain of the familiar Samson. Mine is not the brave leader (who never, after all, actually led his people), nor the Nazirite of God (who, we must admit, was given to whoring and lust), nor just a muscle-bound murderer. For me, this is most of all the story of a man whose life was a never-ending struggle to accommodate himself to the powerful destiny imposed upon him, a destiny he was never able to realise nor, apparently, fully to understand. It is the story of a child who was born a stranger to his father and mother; the story of a magnificent strongman who ceaselessly yearned to win his parents' love – and, therefore, love in general – which in the end he never received.

There are few other Bible stories with so much drama and action, narrative fireworks and raw emotion, as we find in the tale of Samson: the battle with the lion; the three hundred burning foxes; the women he bedded and the one woman that he loved; his betrayal by all the women in his life, from his mother to Delilah; and, in the end, his murderous suicide, when he brought the house down on himself and three thousand Philistines. Yet beyond the wild impulsiveness, the chaos, the din, we can make out a life story that is, at bottom, the tortured journey of a single, lonely and turbulent soul who never found, anywhere, a true home in the world, whose very body was a harsh place of exile. For me, this discovery, this recognition, is the point at which the myth – for all its grand images, its larger-than-life adventures – slips silently into the day-to-day existence of each of us, into our most private moments, our buried secrets.

There is a point in the Samson story – the moment when he falls asleep on Delilah's lap – that seems to absorb and encapsulate the entire tale. Samson withdraws into his childish, almost infantile self, disarmed of the violence, madness, and passion that have confounded and ruined his life. This is, of course, also the moment when his fate is sealed, for Delilah is clutching his hair and the razor, and the Philistines outside are already relishing their victory. In another moment his eyes will be plucked out and his power extinguished. Soon he will be thrown into prison and his days will be ended. Yet it is now, perhaps for the first time in his life, that he finds repose. Here, in the very heart of the cruel perfidy that he has surely expected all along, he is finally granted perfect peace, a release from himself and the stormy drama of his life.

★   ★   ★

In those days, apparently the end of the twelfth and beginning of the eleventh centuries BCE, there was not yet a king in Israel, nor any central authority. The neighbouring nations of Midian, Canaan, Moab, Amon, and Philistia took advantage of the weak Hebrew tribes and launched campaigns of conquest and pillage against them. Every so often there would arise, in one tribe or another, a person who would know how to lead his tribe, sometimes several joined together, into retaliatory battle. If he won, he would become the leader and judge, and be called *shofet*. Such were Gideon and Jephthah, Ehud the son of Gerah, Shamgar the son of Anat, and Deborah, the wife of Lapidot. Thus the Israelites swung cyclically between periods of oppression and redemption that corresponded, as recounted in the Book of Judges, to their sins and their atonement. First they would worship idols, then God would muster the murderous neighbours as punishment. They would cry out to Him in their affliction, and He would elect from among them a person who would save them.

In the midst of this turbulence lived a man and woman of the tribe of Dan. They lived in Zorah in the Judean lowlands, an especially violent region, as in those days it was the boundary between Israel and the Philistines. For the Israelites, it was the first line of defence against the Philistines; for the Philistines, it was the essential first step in any attempt to conquer the Judean hill country. The man was called Manoah, but the woman's name is not known. It is said of her only that she was 'barren and had borne no children', which is enough to suggest that, along with the hardships of the frontier, their marriage had also been filled with pain.

But anyone familiar with the semiotics of biblical storytelling also knows that the very mention of a barren woman almost always foreshadows a momentous birth. And indeed, one day – during one of those periods when 'the Israelites again did what was offensive to the Lord' – when the woman is alone, without her husband, an angel of God appears before her and tells her: 'You are barren and have borne no children; but you shall conceive and bear a son.' And immediately he gives her a list of instructions and warnings, and also good news: 'Now be careful not to drink wine or other intoxicant, or to eat anything unclean; for you are going to conceive and bear a son; let no razor touch his head, for the boy is to be a Nazirite to God from the womb on. It is he who shall begin to deliver Israel from the Philistines.'

She goes to her husband and says, 'A man of God came to me.' And the reader's ears prick up, because the woman does not use the same word as that of the biblical narrator – 'an angel of God *appeared* to the woman' – but rather 'came to me', a charged phrase rich with double meaning, which more than once in the Bible refers to the act of copulation itself.

The husband's ears probably prick up too, and his wife quickly describes the stranger. 'He looked like an angel of God, very frightening,' she explains. 'I did not ask him where he was from, nor did he tell me his name.' And between her words one can hear, it seems, a note of apology – so frightening was the man's appearance that she didn't have the nerve to ask where has was from, or even his name.

And the husband, Manoah, how does he respond, and what does his silence say? Maybe he furrows his brow in puzzlement, trying to fish out a question from the confusion so suddenly thrust upon him by his wife, but she doesn't wait for him to ask, and quickly, anxiously, continues to pile on new information: The man of God told me 'you shall conceive', and promised I would have a son and commanded that I not drink wine or liquor, or eat anything unclean, because the boy would be a Nazirite from the womb until his dying day . . .

There, she has told him everything. She has freed herself from the burden of the encounter and the extraordinary news, yet the text does not tell us a thing about any emotion that flows between them, nor of any smile or tender glance. And this should come as no surprise, since as a rule the Bible rarely records the feelings of its heroes. The Bible is a history of actions and events, and leaves to us, to each and every reader, the task of speculation, an exciting task but one that carries the risks of exaggeration and fantasy. Nevertheless, let us dare to do, in the pages that follow, what many generations of readers before us have done, men and women who have read the spare biblical text according to their faith, the conventions of their age, and their own personal inclinations, and attached meanings and conclusions (and sometimes wishes and delusions) to every word and syllable.[1]

And so, with necessary caution, but also with the pleasure of guesswork and imagination, let us try to fix in our mind's eye the encounter between the man and his wife, she speaking and he listening, she going on at length and he not saying a word. And there is no knowing what is welling under that silence, excitement and joy perhaps, or maybe anger at the wife who converses so freely with a strange man; and we may also wonder whether she, as she speaks, looks him straight in the eye or averts her gaze downward, away from the husband to whom, for some reason, an angel did not appear. And even if only a small part of what we have pictured actually took place, there is no doubt that the news they have received will shake them both to the core, will stir up his deepest feelings about her longtime barrenness and startling pregnancy, and maybe also hers about him, about the weakness and impotence that, it would seem, are hinted at in this brief scene.

And we, peeking in, are so captivated by this highly charged family moment that we almost fail to notice that what the wife reports to her husband is not quite the same as what she had been told. Two central details are missing: she does not mention that a razor must not touch the head of their unborn son, nor does she tell her husband that this son 'shall begin to deliver Israel from the Philistines'.

Why does she omit these crucial details?

One might argue that in her excitement and confusion she simply forgot the matter of the razor. She was doubtless quite agitated; and perhaps assumed that Manoah would be aware that, if the

boy was to be a Nazirite, the well-known restric-
tions would apply, including the prohibition against
the cutting of hair. But how to explain the second
omission? How can it be that a woman withholds –
even conceals – from her husband such significant
information regarding their future son, news that
would surely give him satisfaction and pride, and
perhaps a measure of compensation for all those
bitter, barren years?

To comprehend this, to understand *her*, we need
to go back and read the story through her eyes.
Recall that the biblical text does not even reveal her
name. The word 'barren' is all that is said of her,
and is even redoubled: 'barren and had borne no
children.' And this emphasis suggests that she had
been waiting long years for a child who never arrived.
She has probably given up on the possibility that
she will one day have a child. And it is quite likely
that the 'title' *'akara*, 'the barren one', has been
conferred upon her by others, in the family, in the
tribe, in all of Zorah. And who knows, maybe even
her husband, in moments of anger, flung at her now

and then the searing epithet *'akara*, and between
them, too, the word became her name, the barb that
stings her every time she thinks about herself and
her fate.

And now, this same 'childless one who has not
given birth' is suddenly graced by the appearance of
an angel who brings her the news that she will bear
a child. Yet at this very instant, as her dream is
fulfilled and her joy is boundless, the angel adds: 'For
the boy is to be a Nazirite to God from the womb
on. It is he who shall begin to deliver Israel from the
Philistines.'

And she plunges into a dizzying maelstrom of
thoughts and emotions.

A son will be born to her. To *her*. Until this
moment she knew nothing of this, of course. The
angel knew about it first and told her the news. And
perhaps at the moment of the telling she feels an
unfamiliar twinge inside (angels know that revela-
tions work best with concrete proof). And she is
doubtless very proud that her son will be the one to
save the Israelites: what mother wouldn't be proud

to produce the saviour of his people? But maybe, in a hidden corner of her heart, her happiness is less than complete.

For another recognition, painful and still repressed, is beginning to gnaw at her: she has not conceived her own private, intimate child, but rather some 'national figure', a Nazirite of God and the redeemer of Israel. And his uniqueness is not something that will develop slowly, over the years, so that the two can grow comfortably together into their roles – to be a saviour's mother is also a position of responsibility – but instead this is happening now, suddenly, already, in a fixed and inexorable manner: 'For the boy is to be a Nazirite of God from the womb on . . .'

She tries to understand. This child, this long-awaited child, at the moment he has been given to her, has begun to sprout within her, has already been touched, it turns out, by some other, strange entity, and this means – and here she feels a sharp, alien sting – that he will be a child who will never be hers alone.

Does she understand this immediately? There is no way of knowing. The whole episode has surely overwhelmed her, and it is perfectly possible that at this moment she is filled only with joy over the pregnancy, and pride over the special boy who will be born to her – to *her*, and not to all those in the village and the tribe who saw her only as *'akara*, the childless one . . . But we may surmise that, deep down, Samson's mother knows, with a deep womanly intuition – a knowledge that has nothing to do with any religious faith or fear of God – that what has been given to her has also been taken away in the same instant. The moment of her greatest intimacy – within herself, as a woman – has been confiscated and made into a public event, shared with strangers (including we who interpret her story after thousands of years), and for this reason, in an instinctive gesture of distancing and denial, she pushes away part of the disturbing news.

And here we are reminded of another woman of the Bible, whose fate was the same as that of Samson's mother: Hannah, who tearfully prayed and vowed

that, if a son were born to her, she would give him
to God as a Nazirite, and following that vow, Samuel
was born, and she was obliged to turn him over to
Eli the high priest. Both these tales of extraordinary pregnancies carry with them the uncomfort-
able implication that God has somehow exploited
the despair of these mothers, who thirsted so avidly
to conceive and give birth that they were willing
to accede to any 'suggestion' regarding the destiny
of their child, even – in the language of our own
day – to serve as 'surrogate mothers' for God's
great plans.

\*   \*   \*

The wife of Manoah goes to her husband and tells
him about the encounter, and we have already
observed that her report sounds almost apologetic
and overly detailed: ostensibly revealing all, but in
fact omitting much. It is worth mentioning here that
any number of commentators on the story – including poets and playwrights, painters and novelists

who over the years have explored the character of
Samson – have hinted that Samson was born of a
liaison between his mother and the 'man of God'.
Others, notably Vladimir Jabotinsky in his wonder-
ful novel *Samson the Nazarite*, went so far as to raise
the possibility that Samson was the product of a
romance between his mother and a flesh-and-blood
Philistine.[2] According to this reading, the business
of the 'man of God who came to me' was simply a
cover story that she invented in order to explain
away her embarrassing pregnancy to Manoah. This
hypothesis, of course, adds extra spice to the saga
of Samson's complex relations with the Philistines.
But we, tempted though we are, will trust instead
the version given by Samson's mother, since we shall
soon discover that, even if she spoke the whole truth,
her great, fateful betrayal was not, in the end, at the
expense of her husband.

For, after she announces to Manoah that they will
have a son, she recites to him the second bit of the
angel's message – which, it will be recalled, she
quotes with less than complete accuracy. She omits

to mention the prohibition of hair-cutting; likewise
the boy's future role as national saviour. 'The boy is
to be a Nazirite of God from the womb', she says,
and concludes with a few words of her own: 'until
his dying day'.

And this is surely a strange addendum: a woman,
who has just learned that she will bear a child after
long years of infertility, tells her husband what will
be expected of their son – and then speaks of *his
dying day*?

Even someone who is not a parent, who has never
experienced that special moment at which the
expectant couple gets the good news, knows that
on such an occasion there is nothing farther from
their hearts and minds than the 'dying day' of the
unborn child. And even if many anxious parents are
preoccupied, even to the point of obsession, with
the dangers and disasters that lie in wait for their
children, they are nonetheless not inclined, on the
whole, to imagine their youngster as an elderly
person, decrepit, nearing the end – and certainly
not as dead. To construct such a mental picture

requires a strenuous, almost violent act of estrangement that would appear antithetical to the natural instincts of parenthood.

A woman who thinks and speaks out loud about the dying day of the child that is only beginning to take shape in her womb requires a remarkable measure of grim sobriety. Such a woman, at a moment like this, assumes a posture of cruel alienation – from the child, from the father who hears such words, and, no less, from herself.

What, then, has driven Manoah's wife to add these words?

Again, let's 'rewind the tape' and try to examine what exactly has happened. The angel brings the woman the news, then vanishes. She hurries to her husband, as the mixed message swirls inside her: she is, or will soon become, pregnant; but the child – how to put it? – is not completely hers, is not as other children are to their mothers. He has been deposited within her, as it were, for safekeeping, and she knows that things that are deposited must, in the end, be returned.

Something begins to weigh on her, to slow her down: who, then, is this child that grows within her? Is he wholly made of the essence, the blood and bone, of his parents? If so, why does she faintly sense that even now he is diluted by another essence, foreign and inscrutable, something puzzling and superhuman (and therefore, perhaps, inhuman too)?

Here, in a mental leap forward of several thousand years, what comes to mind is a touching newspaper interview that was once conducted with the mother of Andrei Sakharov, the renowned Russian physicist and Nobel laureate. She spoke of her son with pride, of course, and with love, but at the end of the interview said, with a kind of a sigh: 'Sometimes I feel like a chicken who has given birth to an eagle.' And in those words could be heard a trace of astonishment. One could sense the wonder in her eyes, which distanced the son from the mother's heart and put him in a place where she could look at him with total objectivity, as if he were a 'phenomenon', or an utter stranger: as if the mother herself were putting her son on a high pedestal, and looking at him from the same vantage – the same distance – that any other person might, and from this place she whispers, who are you? How much are you really mine?

And perhaps Samson's mother too, even as she goes to bring her husband the good news, is lacerated by such questions – how much of him is mine? Is this the child I prayed for? Will I be able to give him the bountiful, natural love that for so long I have yearned to give a child of my own?

And then, when she meets her husband and speaks out loud, the words suddenly penetrate her mind with full force, and with all their complex implications. When she reaches the words 'for he will be a Nazirite of God from the womb', it is almost possible to feel how something inside her is blocked, stunned, frozen, and instead of quoting the angel's words completely, she swallows them and blurts out different, unexpected ones, that perhaps took even her by surprise: 'until his dying day'.

And if we have dwelt exhaustively upon this moment, it is because we sense that someone whose mother could look upon him, if only for a moment, from such a distance, whose mother mourned him even before his birth, will always be somewhat alienated and remote in his dealings with others. He will always lack the capacity for simple human contact that comes so naturally to most people, and will never be able to be – as Samson himself phrased it, toward the end of his life – 'an ordinary man'.

And thus, even if Samson's mother has been miraculously 'cured' of her barrenness, it would seem that she has directly passed along to her son the barrenness-as-metaphor that sets a person apart from the vital core of human existence – a unique case of 'hereditary sterility'.

Yet it is God, and not Samson's mother, who has decreed that he will be a Nazirite, in other words, a person who places a partition between himself and life – and indeed in the Hebrew word *nazir* we hear a suggestive conflation of the root *ndr*, meaning 'vow', and the word *zar*, 'stranger'. Nevertheless, it is hard not to feel that it is also the mother's view of her son – her intimate gaze upon the embryo she carries, and her chilling verdict – which no less than God's command has determined the fateful course of his life until his dying day.

*　　*　　*

The strangeness conferred upon the unborn child is soon multiplied. Manoah, taken by surprise, prays to God and requests further instructions: 'Oh, my Lord! Please let the man of God that You sent come to us again and let him instruct us how to act with the boy that is to be born.'

'*The boy* that is to be born?' Still in his mother's womb, Samson is already classified by his father, assigned a formal, arm's-length definition. For even if Manoah's lips have longed for many years to pronounce the words 'our son', 'my child', 'my boy', he takes care to use the term used by the man of God as quoted by his wife, perhaps because he senses that he must, even now, maintain an awestruck distance from one who will soon be an exalted figure.

DAVID GROSSMAN

And Manoah perhaps guesses something more: that it will be necessary to handle this child like a precious vessel – maybe too precious – which is possibly beyond the spiritual means of its own parents; and that this will not be a child who can be raised according to one's natural instincts alone; and God, I beg of you, kindly furnish additional instructions . . .

And indeed, the angel returns, but again chooses to appear before the wife as 'she was sitting in the field and her husband Manoah was not with her'. And thus the impression is strengthened that the angel for some reason prefers to entrust the information, the secret, to the woman, and that he endeavours to meet with her when she is alone, and not merely 'alone', but when her husband is not with her. But she – perhaps for fear of gossip, or out of loyalty to her husband and a sense of their shared destiny – wants Manoah to be present at the meeting. This time, the narrator goes into a bit of detail: 'The woman ran in haste to tell her husband.' And we can imagine her strong legs racing through the stalks of corn, her arms pumping, slicing the air, the thoughts flying through her head, as she reaches Manoah and tells him that the same man, 'the man who came to me before', has appeared to her once again.

*Vayakom vayelech Manoah aharei ishto*: 'Manoah rose and followed his wife.'

The ring and resonance of these words convey the slow, heavy movements of Manoah, whose name means 'rest' and, in more recent Hebrew, also means 'late', in the sense of 'deceased'. Thus, in five words that stand in amusing contrast to 'the woman ran in haste to tell her husband', the narrator sketched a sluggard of sorts who drags after his quick, energetic wife. Indeed Manoah was chastised by the rabbinic authors of the Talmud, who labelled him an *am ha'aretz*, an ignoramus, for transgressing a cardinal rule of gender: 'A man does not walk behind a woman on the road, even his own wife – and, even if he finds himself on a bridge with her, she should be beside him, and whoever walks behind a woman when crossing a river will have no share in the world to come.'[3]

So Manoah follows his wife, meets the stranger, attempts to size him up. Although he had earlier explicitly requested that the Almighty bring back the 'man of God', Manoah may not yet be free of a nagging suspicion about the fellow whom his wife met alone in the field – twice – after which she knew immediately that she was to bear a child. 'Are you the man who spoke to my wife?' he demands, and the reader can imagine, beyond the words, the dejected look he directs at the angel, and hear the mixture of mistrust and jealousy and the irritable humility of a man who cannot help but recognise his own inferiority.

Note that Manoah does not ask 'Are you the man who *came* to my wife?' Perhaps something restrains him from using that blunt word, whose utterance in such a charged setting – two men, one possibly pregnant woman – could well push the three into out-and-out confrontation. Yet at the same time, Manoah calls the stranger a 'man' and not 'the man of God', and juxtaposes the words 'man' and 'wife', coupling the two in an intimate cocoon while he stands outside, thus exposing further his suspicions and the jealousy that flickers behind his question.[4]

And the angel answers, curtly: 'I am.'

'May your words soon come true,' says Manoah, adding: 'What rules shall be observed for the boy?' And here again there seeps an undertone of wariness toward the stranger, and maybe toward the promised son too, and it is clear that Manoah still does not believe he is conversing with a man of God, much less an *angel*, for if he did he would surely fling himself upon the ground and not speak to him as he has, with a lack of courtesy and not one word of supplication.

And here arises the question: has the angel changed his appearance in between his two 'performances', before the wife and now the husband? For it is clear that in Manoah's eyes he does not appear unmistakably to be 'an angel of God, very frightening'. Did the woman exaggerate, for some reason, in her description – or perhaps the angel's appearance has not changed at all, but rather the real difference lies in the abilities of the man and the woman to 'read' the hidden identity of their interlocutor?

The angel, once again, provides detailed instructions regarding the right conduct that will ensure the proper birth and rearing of God's Nazirite. At the same time, it is hard not to notice that, throughout the conversation, he speaks to Manoah with obvious reluctance, as if under protest, thus emphasising the man's superfluousness, his second-class status in relation to his wife: 'The woman must abstain from all the things against which I warned her.'

Upon re-reading we notice that the angel too, when he repeats the instructions to Manoah, does not mention the prohibition against cutting the child's hair. What is the meaning of this repeated omission, this time on the angel's part? When the woman did so, it could be attributed to her temporary confusion. But this time the omission takes on a more serious aspect: Samson's weak spot was, of course, his hair, and the shearing of his locks was what, in the end, brought about his death. Can it be that the woman and the angel wished, for some reason, to conceal from the father the secret of the son's weakness? Is it possible that that the two of them sensed that in a matter so critical to the life of 'the child that is to be born' Manoah could not be relied upon to keep the secret?

Even after the outlining of the instructions, the tension between the husband and the angel continues. Manoah's situation is intolerable: a sea of information overwhelms him from every side; he is flooded by harsh, conflicting feelings, foremost the nagging suspicion that his wife and the haughty stranger are weaving an elaborate conspiracy against him. Even someone far quicker and cleverer would feel, at a moment like this, that his mind was growing dim. In his distress, Manoah attempts to draw closer to the angel: 'Let us detain you and prepare a kid for you,' he offers. The angel declines, for no apparent reason, in a hostile and judgmental manner: 'If you detain me, I shall not eat your food,' he says, adding that Manoah should sacrifice the kid to God, not to him. Maybe he suspects that Manoah merely wants to detain him, in order to try to figure him out. 'For Manoah did not know that he was an angel of the Lord,' reads the text, and this lack of knowledge, even after a few minutes have gone by, further attests to the dullness of Manoah's character.

Embarrassed, Manoah asks the angel's name, appending a clumsy explanation to his question: 'We should like to honour you when your words come true,' in other words, when your prophecy comes to pass. But the angel rebuffs him: 'You must not ask for my name; it is *peli*,' miraculous, unknowable. '*Peli*,' he retorts; in other words, beyond your ken, too big for you. One can assume that this word, spoken out of a clear desire to silence Manoah, will long be etched in his memory. An insult like this cannot but echo in days to come, when he will face his son and will run into – as into a wall – his unfathomable, strange, miraculous deeds.

Manoah, hesitant and confused following the angel's off-putting reply, places the kid and the meal offering on the rock. The angel performs a miracle, produces fire from the rock, and then ascends heavenward as Manoah and his wife watch and fling themselves face downwards on the ground. And only now, finally, does Manoah believe that indeed this was an angel of God. 'We shall surely die, for we have seen a divine being,' he tells his wife, his voice quivering with fear – a fear not only of God and angel but of everything that the astonishing encounter is destined to bring about in their lives. And maybe it is also a fear of the unborn child, their child, for whom they had waited and prayed, who even now is surrounded not only by amniotic fluid but by an impenetrable membrane of enigma and menace.

'We will surely die,' mumbles Manoah, and his wife responds with simple logic, perhaps also with subtle scorn that she draws from the angel's air of chilly condescension, which still hovers over them: 'Had the Lord meant to take our lives, He would not have accepted a burnt offering and meal offering from us, nor let us see all these things, and He would not have made such an announcement to us.'

And so, this woman, who until moments earlier had been reducible to the epithet 'the childless one', grows larger in the reader's mind with every passing verse. Perhaps it is the new pregnancy that empowers and ennobles her, or perhaps what instils new confidence, despite all her doubts and anxieties, is the knowledge that she carries a child who is one of a kind. It is hard to imagine, moreover, that a woman as sharp as she is had failed to notice that the angel opted – twice – to appear to her alone.

But it may also be that these guesses are incorrect, confusing cause and effect; and it is rather that she has been this way all along, a strong and quick-witted woman, resourceful and brave, and precisely for these reasons the angel preferred to bring her, and not her husband, the news. It is interesting to note in this connection that Rembrandt, when he drew the encounter between the couple and the angel, 'pushed' Manoah face down into a submissive, even ridiculous position – at first glance he resembles a sack of potatoes – whereas the wife, in contrast to the biblical account, sits erect beside her fallen husband, exuding nobility, confidence, and determination. It is clear that Rembrandt too,

---

grows larger in the reader's mind with every passing verse. Perhaps it is the new pregnancy that empowers and ennobles her, or perhaps what instils new confidence, despite all her doubts and anxieties, is the knowledge that she carries a child who is one of a kind. It is hard to imagine, moreover, that a woman as sharp as she is had failed to notice that the angel opted – twice – to appear to her alone.

But it may also be that these guesses are incorrect, confusing cause and effect; and it is rather that she has been this way all along, a strong and quick-witted woman, resourceful and brave, and precisely for these reasons the angel preferred to bring her, and not her husband, the news. It is interesting to note in this connection that Rembrandt, when he drew the encounter between the couple and the angel, 'pushed' Manoah face down into a submissive, even ridiculous position – at first glance he resembles a sack of potatoes – whereas the wife, in contrast to the biblical account, sits erect beside her fallen husband, exuding nobility, confidence, and determination. It is clear that Rembrandt too, like many who have read the story, sensed that the woman is the strong, dominant one. And if this is so, we can already imagine how decisive her influence, and that of the words she has just spoken, will be upon Samson – from the womb until his dying day.

* * *

Zorah today is a kibbutz, located not far from a *tel*, or mound, that almost certainly sits atop the archaeological remains of the biblical settlement. Its founders, members of the socialist 'United Kibbutz' movement and veterans of the legendary Palmach fighting force, settled there towards the end of 1948, in the midst of the War of Independence that had broken out when the armies of four Arab countries invaded the newborn State of Israel. During this war, as in the wars in the time of the Judges, the Judean lowlands were of great strategic importance and therefore a focus of the warring forces. When the Israeli army drew near the Arab village of Sar'a, most of its inhabitants fled, and the ones who remained were expelled. All became refugees, most of whom ended up in the Deheishe refugee camp not far from Hebron, where their families reside to this day.

It is mid-October 2002. A hot, gloomy day in the lowlands. The radio reports heavy traffic at the Samson Junction, between Zorah and Eshtaol. A dirt path winds away from the main highway into a forest, leading the hiker into the abandoned gardens of Arab Sar'a. There, hidden in a small grove, suddenly appear two figures, a mother and son, Palestinians who have come from Deheishe to harvest the olives from trees that once belonged to their family. The woman vigorously shakes the branches of the tree and beats at them with a stick, and her son, a boy of about ten, swiftly and silently gathers the black hail of olives on a sheet spread out beneath the tree.

Here, roughly three thousand years ago, in this same brown, rugged landscape, amidst olive and oak trees, terebinths and carobs, the wife of Manoah lay down to give birth. Here she gave the boy his name, *Shimshon*, which in Hebrew connotes 'little sun', and perhaps also a conflation of *shemesh* and *on* – sun plus strength, virility.

There is, of course, great similarity between Samson and other 'sun-heroes' such as Hercules, Perseus, Prometheus and Mopsus, son of Apollo.[5] In the Talmud, Rabbi Yohanan sought to 'purify' Samson of any hint of paganism: 'Samson was called by the name of the Holy One, Blessed be He, as it is said, 'For the Lord God is a sun and a shield' (Psalms 84:12) . . . as God protects the entire world, so too Samson in his time protects Israel.'[6] Whereas the first-century Judeo-Roman historian Josephus Flavius, in his *Jewish Antiquities*, asserts that 'Samson' means 'strong', adding that 'the child grew apace and it was plain from the frugality of his diet and his loosely flowing locks that he was to be a prophet'.[7]

'The boy grew up, and the Lord blessed him', the Bible tells us, and the Talmud comments, 'He was blessed *b'amato*', the word *amah* (literally, 'cubit') being a euphemism for penis: 'His *amah* was like that of other men', continues the Talmud, 'but his seed was like a fast-flowing stream'.[8] Even if this rabbinic commentary ventures fancifully far afield, Samson's subsequent deeds do substantiate the general thrust of its assumption. And no less important than this particular divine blessing is what comes thereafter: 'The spirit of the Lord began to move him in the encampment of Dan, between Zorah and Eshtaol.'

What exactly is this divine 'spirit' that begins to 'move' the lad? Was it a sense of mission, a calling, or an interior burst of inspiration? *Lefa'amo*, reads the Hebrew, from the root 'to beat' or 'throb', a clear echo of the human heartbeat, which pounds louder as one's emotions are stirred. Indeed this sound, persistent and agitated, will surge from Samson's body and soul at every stage of his life. The Jerusalem Talmud, attempting to give concrete physical expression to Samson's arousal, declares that, when the holy spirit came upon him, each of his footsteps was as great as the distance from Zorah to Eshtaol, and the locks of his hair would ring like a bell – *pa'amon* in Hebrew, from that same root – and the sound would carry for that distance as well.[9] The *Zohar* or 'Book of Splendour', the central work of Jewish mysticism, offers an appealingly vivid description: '*Lefa'amo.* The spirit would come and go, come and go, and never properly settle within him. And it is therefore written, "The spirit of the Lord began to move him," for this was the case from the beginning.'[10] The medieval commentator Gersonides, in another play on words, interprets Samson's arousal from the hero's rational point of view: 'One time (*pa'am*) he would decide to go to war against the Philistines, another time he would decide not to, like a bell that strikes this way and that.'

Yet a simple reading of the text reveals that Samson is not stirred by any calling or inspiration but rather in a different, unexpected direction. For what does the young man do when he is aroused by the spirit of God? Does he begin gathering an army in order to redeem his people as soon as possible from the Philistines, or amass political power within his tribe, or try to get the blessing and support of a high priest? Not at all: Samson awakens to *love*.

'Samson went down to Timnah; and while in Timnah, he noticed a girl among the Philistine women.'

Straight away he goes back up the hill, home to Zorah, turns to his father and mother, and declares: 'I noticed one of the Philistine women in Timnah; now get her for me as a wife.' And although the word 'love' is not stated here explicitly, one can sense in Samson's words the determination and depth of feeling that churn inside him. It is hard to know if he himself is capable at this moment of differentiating his tangled emotions, of separating love from the great new 'divine spirit', but is this so surprising? Love, and first love all the more, is doubtless likely to arouse in a person the sense that he has just been born and that a new, powerful, and unfamiliar wind is coursing through him.

Here is the place to explain – for those who puzzle over this speedy coupling of a Nazirite with a woman – that the Nazirite in Judaism is not the same as a monk in the Christian or Buddhist traditions.[11] In the Torah (see Numbers, Chapter 6), the Jewish Nazirite is commanded to refrain from three things: he is forbidden to drink wine or to eat grapes or their derivatives; he may not cut his hair; and he may not go near a dead body (a prohibition not specified in the case of Samson). On the other hand, he is not forbidden to marry or to be intimate with a woman. Still, the reader is advised not to harbour expectations of juicy escapades akin to the tales of lecherous monks in Chaucer or Boccaccio. The biblical writer – who, like most authors, is a natural-born killjoy – is quick to remark, regarding Samson's attraction to the Philistine woman, 'that this was the Lord's doing; He was seeking a pretext against the Philistines, for the Philistines were ruling over Israel at that time.'

In other words – not love, or lust, or romance, and above all not free will: Samson is drawn to the Philistine woman because God is looking for an excuse to strike the Philistines who are oppressing the Israelites. This is the sole motive the Bible offers for the desire that Samson feels. But this presenta-tion of events cannot prevent the reader from wondering about the role of Samson *the man* in this story. For he himself surely does not experience his feelings of love as someone else's 'pretext' – not even God's – and his strong and immediate reaction to the woman from Timnah proves that he, the man, the flesh-and-blood Samson, seeks and needs love! Is he in any way capable of understanding that this burning love is not entirely 'his', and that he is merely a political and military tool in God's hands? Is there any man who could understand such a thing? Is there anyone who could endure the knowledge that, just as he was not his parents' 'natural child', so too now, as a man, his natural desire for a woman has been confiscated, or else installed in him?

And as we raise these questions, a sad possibility becomes increasingly apparent: that the hero of our story is a man who does not know, and perhaps will never really understand, that God, even before his birth, has *nationalised* his desires, his love, his entire emotional life.

'Get her for me as a wife,' Samson half-asks, half-demands of his parents. It is interesting to note that, in contrast with the typical biblical scene in which a son asks his father to bring him a particular woman as a wife, here Samson takes his request to both his father and mother. And from here on, they will almost always be mentioned together, the father and the mother, as again and again the biblical storyteller makes it clear that Samson's mother is at least as important as his father.

And they also answer him together, in one voice ('His father and mother said to him'), what parents typically say to Samsons in such situations: 'Is there no one among the daughters of your own kinsmen and among all our people, that you must go and take a wife from the uncircumcised Philistines?' In other words – why don't you marry one of our own?

For it is not only that Samson chooses to marry a foreigner, the daughter of another people, but that this particular people, the Philistines, are among the worst and bitterest of Israel's foes: with the advantage of iron weapons they repeatedly engage in the conquest and enslavement of the tribes of Israel, while preventing them from developing iron-smithing of their own, 'for the Philistines were afraid that the Hebrews would make swords or spears'.[12] Indeed for the past forty years, as is told in the beginning of our story, they have dominated and provoked the Israelites. And it is also known that the tribe of Dan, Samson's tribe, dwells in the borderlands and finds it hard to build a homestead there, as it is continually embattled with stronger nations, the Philistines and others. These continued struggles have exhausted the tribe, depleted it and stripped it of cultural, political, and social influence within the Israelite nation.[13] (In this light it is pos-sible to read as somewhat unrealistic the blessing of Dan by his father Jacob before the patriarch's death, the expression of both a hope and a wish: 'Dan shall govern his people as one of the tribes of Israel.' After which Jacob adds, perhaps with a heavy sigh: 'I wait for your deliverance, O Lord . . .')[14]

This is the larger national context in which the

relationship between Samson and the Philistine woman begins to blossom. But no less fascinating is what happens here between the young man and his parents: first of all, they are confused, because they know (or at least his mother does) that Samson is destined to save his people from the Philistines, so what is he doing with a Philistine woman? Next, when they say to him, 'Is there no one among the daughters of your own kinsmen and among all our people, that you must go and take a wife from the uncircumcised Philistines?' there is a clear echo of blame and complaint: 'Why can't you be like everyone else?' We may read this with a smile, as it sounds like one of those tired lines so many of us have heard from our parents (and sworn never to say to our children), but the Samson story is anything but a comedy. It is a tragic tale; not least because the strangeness of *this* child, his difference from his parents, is so sharp and clear-cut that it sometimes seems that he and they belong to two entirely different dimensions of human existence, realms that are separated by an unbridgeable chasm. And therefore, that trite parental line is uttered here with incurable, heart-rending anguish.

For it can be assumed that by now Samson's parents have gathered that, with every step he takes, his strangeness and otherness will become more and more pronounced, that it will become clear to one and all that he, in a sense, is made of different 'stuff' – from some alien, unknowable essence that infiltrated him even in the womb – on account of which he will never, in all likelihood, be able to connect naturally and harmoniously with his family or his people.

And even though they know well – having been the ones, after all, who were given the news – that Samson, by his nature, cannot be 'like everyone else' or like other human beings, they blurt out the plaintive question because it is so hard for them, as parents, to finally come to terms, without hesitation, with the grand divine plan that confiscated their son and made him what he is. They feel, both of them, the pain of the umbilical cord so roughly torn, which will stay sundered forever.

One can imagine that at this moment – as his

parents try to protest his decision – Samson looks straight into his father's eyes. He wants to make it clear to him, with that look, just how 'right' this woman is, in his opinion. Facing him is the indecisive, fearful Manoah. Manoah, ever suspicious of this son who hatched so suddenly in his nest, like the chick of a strange bird, unexpected and dangerous. Manoah – a man so utterly unlike his energetic, obsessive, determined, brave, and excitable son, Samson. According to the text, Samson does not respond to his father's and mother's question. We don't know if this is because he is indeed so determined, or whether that pained parental query – 'Is there no one among the daughters of your own kinsmen and among all our people, that you must go and take a wife from the uncircumcised Philistines?' – triggers, for a second, an unsettling sensation, the vague glimmer of possibility that the reason he is so attracted to this Philistine girl may not be so obvious, or entirely 'natural'.

Again he says to Manoah: 'Get me that one, for she is the right one for me.' This time, Samson only addresses his father. Possibly he does so because he senses that Manoah is weaker and more easily swayed. But it may also be that he feels compelled to avert his eyes from his mother, for when he speaks about a woman who is 'the right one', he is incapable of looking straight at the woman who was a senior partner– if an unwilling one – in ordaining his tangled, troublesome destiny.

Samson and his father exchange duelling glances. This is a decisive moment in Samson's personal history. Other difficult struggles await him, but this is the first time he has had to rebel openly against his father's authority (and his mother's). Without a doubt it has been abundantly clear to everyone, even before this situation, that Samson is not the same as other people. Stories told within the family and spread among the tribe have buttressed this impression, stories about the unusual circumstances of his conception and the exalted task for which he has been chosen. His long hair, too, which has never been cut, has singled him out before one and all as *sui generis*. But this, now, is the moment when Samson declares himself not merely different, but also to be someone who is closer in his soul to the foreigner, the enemy.

*    *    *

They are on their way. Samson, his father and his mother have set out from Zorah towards the woman from Timnah, on trails that wind through dry brambles and late-summer fields of dusty stubble.

Long-legged Samson walks in broad strides, drawn towards Timnah by a powerful force. Ordinary mortals would find it hard to keep pace with him. His parents doubtless need to stop now and again and catch their breath; here, for example, on a hilltop at the southwest crest of the Zorah ridge, overlooking the valley of Nahal Sorek, they stand, take a breath, wipe their sweaty faces. In those days the area was thickly wooded – 'as plentiful as sycamores in the Shephelah plain'[15] was once a simile for abundance – but today the trees are sparse, the hills exposed. The sycamores have been replaced by pines,

— 47 —

planted by the Jewish National Fund, which in the thick air of a Levantine sirocco look almost grey. Below, in the plain, lies the city of Beit Shemesh, with its roads and rooftops and industrial zones, and the flat drainage basins of the surrounding streams, sparkling like mirrors, and something flaming red-orange in the distance – maybe a tree has caught fire in the searing *hamsin* wind, or maybe it's just burning garbage – and Samson's back disappears over the saddle of the ridge, into the valley, down to Timnah.

And here, at the entrance to the vineyards of Timnah, a roaring lion appears before him, one of those that were indigenous to the Land of Israel in those days, but have since become extinct. The divine spirit then descends upon Samson: quick as a wink he tears the lion apart 'as one might tear a kid asunder'. He does so with his bare hands, 'but he did not tell his father and mother what he had done'.

Two things cry out here for interpretation: how is it possible that his parents didn't witness the battle? This puzzle can be solved with perfectly simple explanations: he was walking faster than they were; he knew a shortcut but they were on the main road; or maybe, while his parents walked through the vineyards of Timnah, he circumvented them so as not to transgress the Nazirite prohibition against any contact with grapes.[16]

The second question is more difficult: he is walking along with his parents, tears a lion limb from limb with his bare hands, and says nothing. Why is he silent? Out of modesty? Or perhaps he considers the event insignificant? Hard to believe, not only because the feat itself is so extraordinary, but because it will quickly become apparent that Samson keeps replaying it in his mind, and even boasting about it.

Then maybe he is silent because he senses that the episode with the lion doesn't 'connect' with his relationship to his parents, or with his relations with human beings in general? In other words, it's possible that Samson senses that the battle with the lion is some sort of sign, part of a secret code in which he communicates with that 'divine spirit' within him; a sort of sign-language through which God reconfirms the special bond between them, and

DAVID GROSSMAN

instructs him to stay the course and trust the impulses that guide him, even when they contradict his parents' wishes.

Because what he has done to the lion is so vastly beyond any human scale, is it possible that Samson is simply *wary* of involving his parents, so as not to give them further proof of just how different he is, and alien to them? For someone like him understands too well that every additional piece of evidence will distance his parents from him a little more, and each of these progressive acts of distancing – even as they are vital signs of his uniqueness – are deeply painful, cutting him off bit by bit, culminating in utter exile.

And it's also a possibility that what he has discovered about *himself*, while battling the lion, has frightened him: the hidden superhuman power that has burst out and revealed itself to him for the first time has, perhaps, also shocked him and created a partition between Samson and his new, larger-than-life self that does not fully belong to the human race.

And perhaps someone seen by his parents as a

stranger when he was still in the womb, who even then was deprived of full parental approval, is fated to be forever a little suspicious of himself. Wary of a strange and inscrutable aspect of his being, an aspect that is – exactly like the angel who brought his parents the news – 'miraculous', mysterious and unknowable, and therefore a continuing source of wonder and doubt. And it's possible to go a step further, and gather that someone who is thus sentenced to self-doubt is likely to be uncertain not only about whether he is the legitimate child of his parents: there also remains that faint, lingering doubt as to whether he is a 'legitimate' member of the human family altogether, whether he is 'like other people', and this corrosive uncertainty is something he can never shed. There will always be a stranger inside him, a hidden, hostile passenger – perhaps even a fifth column, a saboteur.

\*　　\*　　\*

He arrives in Timnah, and again meets the Philistine

woman, and no doubt quietly looks her up and down, to confirm that she is to his taste (and also pays close attention to his parents' reactions to her). And again the narrator emphasises, after this encounter too, that 'she pleased Samson', she was 'right' for him. Meanwhile the reader, who knows that this new love is nothing other than a divinely selected pretext for striking back at the Philistines, contemplates the sad disparity between Samson's romantic impulses and what God intends to make of them.

When Samson, 'after a while', comes back to marry the woman, he returns to see 'the remains of the lion'. He doesn't merely return, but 'turned aside to see the remains' – in other words, he has detoured from his path to his future wife in order to look once more at the dead lion.

It's not difficult, of course, to empathise with him, to understand his need to go back and relish the hour of glory that remains sealed secretly inside him. But one can also imagine that he goes there because, as the days have passed (and 'days' here might well mean a whole year), even he himself has begun to doubt whether indeed this great thing actually happened to him, or whether it was only a dream. Or does he simply feel a need to return to the place where he scored his grand victory, in order to reconfirm his manliness before he goes to the woman?

And then, as he stands before the dead lion, he sees 'in the lion's skeleton a swarm of bees and honey, and scooped it into his palms'.[17] Samson, a grown man – nowhere in the text is he described as a giant – stands in wonder at the sight. Before his eyes, bees buzz around the skeleton. Honey has accumulated inside the lion. Samson extends his hand – without fear of the bees – and scoops honey into his mouth, and it touches the reader's heart as he reaches out so simply, innocently, sponta-neously: he sees, he wants, he takes . . . And just as he killed the lion with his bare hands, so too does he scoop out the honey from inside it, not with a ladle or into a jar, but with his *hands*, and then 'ate it as he went along. When he rejoined his father and mother, he gave them some and they ate it; but he did not tell them that he had scooped the honey out of a lion's skeleton.'

Take a look at him: a he-man with a little licking boy inside. (How astonishing and poignant, this gulf between enormous physical strength and an immature, childlike soul.) He walks and eats, walks and licks, till he gets home to mum and dad, and gives them the honey, 'and they ate it', apparently straight from the palms of his hands. What a marvellous, sensual scene!

But would it be too much to imagine that Samson, walking and licking the honey, begins to discern something entirely new? Something that will be woven into the fabric of his life from now on, which breaks through as Samson heads home, a private revelation of sorts that is bound up with the sight of the lion's skeleton and the taste of the honey, and also the linkage of these sensations with the feelings aroused in him by the woman to whom he is going . . .

For it is likely that when Samson saw this remarkable sight, the honey in the lion, he was pierced by a new, almost prophetic intuition, something born inside him as he absorbed the immense symbolic significance of such a powerful image. Something connected in an altogether new way with perception, with a way of looking at reality, indeed something akin to a world-view.

He looks at the lion and the honey pooling inside it. Certainly he is strongly affected: after all, this image will figure in the riddle he will soon pose at his wedding party. He sees the extraordinary scene that he himself created: it was he who killed the lion. Because of him the bees built their hive there and made their honey, the sweet honey that now fills his mouth . . . and as his senses blend one into the other, is it not probable that he becomes spontaneously excited over something that is a powerful sight, oddly beautiful, utterly unique, and that also radiates a sense of deep, hidden, symbolic meaning?

How to define such a moment? We have already called it 'revelation'. But may we cautiously add that this is also the moment at which Samson, the consummate strongman, suddenly discovers the way in which an *artist* looks at the world?

And if it seems peculiar, at this stage of the story, to describe Samson as an artist, it is from this moment onward, from his encounter with the lion's honey, that he will display a clear tendency to mould reality – whatever reality he may come in contact with – and stamp it with his own unique signature, and, one might add, his *style*.

And even if Samson is not an artist in any traditional or classical sense, it is possible that at this moment, facing the remains of the lion, he senses that there is a clue hidden here for him. A clue that leads to a new and unfamiliar dimension of reality, or at least a new way of seeing it that is more than just passive observation, but contains the powers of creation and renewal – triggered in him, perhaps, by the humming of life inside the skeleton – and through which he can mitigate, without sacrificing his singularity, the strange loneliness into which he was born.

He goes on his way, honey dripping from his palms, heads home to mum and dad, a giant child, hiding secrets, feeding them from his hands, 'but he

did not tell them that he had scooped the honey out
of a lion's skeleton'. In other words, even now he
does not tell them how he tore the lion apart, or
where he got the honey. And no less amazing: they
don't ask him a thing. Maybe they are afraid to ask.
Afraid of an answer that might expose the yawning
chasm between them.

Because they keep silent, he does too. Maybe he
hopes that something will become clear to them,
without words or even a hint on his part. That they
will guess (the way kids always hope their parents
will find them out): they'll float some theory, say,
regarding the source of the honey, or they'll make a
joke about the unusual scent of this sticky stuff, and
along the way, with sudden, sharp intuition, they
will also guess something about Samson himself,
about their son's true self, which has been hidden or
withheld from them.

With all that, despite the heavy silence, or
maybe because of it, there is also something
mischievous, full of *joie de vivre* and even humour,
to be found in this family moment, which has no

parallel anywhere in the Bible: They say nothing, do not ask, he doesn't tell, and nevertheless it is so appealing to imagine Samson waving his hands high, and his parents, doubtless smaller than he is, jumping at him with mouths wide open and tongues hanging out, and Samson howling with glee, playing with his parents, touching them and dancing for them and laughing with them like any normal person, with the honey dripping, flowing down a cheek, sliding to the chin, being licked up, as the laughter swells to the point of tears . . .

With these drops of honey he is telling them something that apparently he can tell them no other way. And – incidentally – it was so urgent for him to tell them this that he forgot where he was going: he had, we recall, been on his way to Timnah! What had happened to him, that all of a sudden he turned around and headed home, to father and mother? Did he suddenly forget he was on his way to take a wife? (And here, of course, the words of Gersonides again ring true: Samson was 'like a bell that strikes this way and that'.)

And in this spontaneous, almost instinctive action, we can clearly see the extent to which he oscillates between the desire to leave his parents and build a life as a mature adult, and his yearning to be with them, to win their approval again and again. The umbilical cord that connects them will continue to stretch and contract throughout the entire story. And maybe precisely because that cord, from the beginning, had joined Samson and his mother in so unorthodox a fashion, the bond was never susceptible to being cut in a natural way. And already here we wonder – is this not the ambivalence that will prevent Samson, throughout his life, from ever falling in love with a woman who can truly sever that umbilical cord and tie him to herself in a natural manner, as man is tied to wife?

But this question will be asked in due time. Meanwhile, Samson is still with them, with his parents, and they are eating the honey from his cupped hands. And as we said, for Samson it is perhaps the very honey that was scooped from inside the lion, this 'lionised' honey, which makes concrete

what he never knew how to put into words, what he
always yearned to explain to his parents: that they
should understand that he – despite the destiny that
was decreed in the womb, which cut him off from
them and appropriated his life for some hidden divine
purpose, and notwithstanding his huge muscles and
incomparable strength – he still very much needs
their understanding, their love, their repeated
approval. 'Here, look,' he is saying in effect to them,
as they suckle his fingers, 'look what I have inside,
under all these muscles, muscles like a lion's, and
under this mane I am forbidden to cut; and under
this mission, too, which has been imposed upon me,
this regal fate to which I have been sentenced. Look
inside me. Just once, look deep inside me, and you
will finally see that "out of the strong came something sweet".'

And his father and mother continue to lick the
honey from his hands, but now, as the playfulness
and laughter start to fade, the old uneasiness begins
to gnaw at them. They can't look straight at him
because he, it would seem, was never quite right with

them. Of course they sense his need and desire to be close to them – a simple, homey, familial close-ness – and they, too, want to be with him, and sense his love for them, and wish, like every parent, to love their child with all their hearts; but there is always that barrier. Something that gets in the way. Something that doubtless makes him someone worthy of pride, but not fully understood. Important, but not quite loved.

And there is also their clear realisation that he will not accept their authority. Not in the matter of the Philistine woman he insists on marrying, nor apparently in any other matter, because he is subject to the authority of a power greater than theirs. And they know painfully, even with a sense of shame, that he is fated to make his way alone in life, along his own path that resembles no other, and that they can't teach him a thing. Nothing in their lives or experi-ence has prepared them to be the parents of such a person. Even this honey – which came from God knows where – they taste half-heartedly, sensing that a secret is dripping out here but unable to fathom it any more than they can decipher what their son is trying to tell them.

And precisely because of their limited understanding of him, we get a strong feeling that Samson wants to calm their anxiety about him and the oppressive mystery hidden within him. He envelops them in sweetness and tries to bind them to him with the sticky honey, and he pleads with them to believe in him and trust him and be completely certain that he is really theirs, that they are really his parents despite the abnormal circumstances surrounding his conception, and that he, in his strange way, is loyal to them.

For there is betrayal in the air. It is unspoken, undefined; nor is it necessarily a 'typical' betrayal, of the sort commonly imputed to Samson's birth – his mother cheating on his father with the mysterious stranger – but possibly deeper and more destructive. For if you have a child who is suffused, even in his mother's womb, with a sense of strangeness – perhaps there was a flinching, an instinctive rejection as fleeting as a single contraction of the uterus around the embryo – and if there is always wonder and fear and even suspicion of the child and what may erupt from him: if all these hover in the family air, there is a permanent feeling of betrayal. To be more specific, a sense of being betrayed. Hidden, deep, *mutual*. None of them wanted it, of course, but so it was decreed, for all three. And Samson will live with this feeling all his life, and all his actions will be dedicated to understanding this feeling at close range, or grieving over it, or replaying it over and over.

Three people in the world. A couple whose son was 'nationalised' even before his birth. A son who is born, in effect, an orphan. How difficult is Samson's twofold, self-contradictory mission in life: to be himself, with all his unusual inclinations, and at the same time, to be faithful to the parents from whom he differs so much. We'll leave them for now: all the honey in the world cannot sweeten the moment.

★   ★   ★

Samson goes back down to Timnah, to get married. This time he goes there with his father alone, and we wonder, was this the custom, or did his mother decide, for some reason, not to participate in her son's wedding ceremony? And if so, how should we interpret this blunt gesture? Is this her way of protesting against Samson's decision to disobey her and marry the Philistine woman? Or perhaps she refused to give her consent to the marriage because she felt, with her sharp motherly intuition, that nothing good would come of this, not necessarily because of the bride but because her son, Samson, for subtle reasons she cannot express in words but recognises nonetheless, is not the marrying kind?

'And Samson made a feast there, as young men used to do.'

Here, muses the reader, here at last Samson is trying to do something 'like everyone else'. But it turns out that even this simple wish is destined to go bad quickly: when the Philistines see him, they choose thirty *mere'im*, 'companions', to accompany Samson during the wedding feast. Why they do so, we do not know, but it would seem that his appearance, his obvious strength, and perhaps also an air of disquiet and wildness that he carries with him always, prompt them to surround him this way, to prevent any trouble. The narrator does not say who these companions are, but it is fairly obvious that a man like Samson has no *friends*, not even at his wedding, but rather *mere'im* (the very sound of which, implying the Hebrew word *ra* – evil – does not bode well).

No sooner does the wedding feast begin than Samson sets his guests a challenge: 'Let me pose you a riddle,' he says. 'If you can give me the right answer during the seven days of the feast, I shall give you thirty linen tunics and thirty sets of clothing; but if you are not able to tell me it, you must give me thirty linen tunics and thirty sets of clothing.'

And when they agree to the conditions, he poses the riddle: 'Out of the eater came something to eat/ Out of the strong came something sweet.'

In point of fact, almost every time Samson opens his mouth a surprising bit of poetry pops out. After

all, as his actions testify, he is a man who inspires
fear and repulsion: a bully capable of unlimited
mayhem and destruction, who leaves a trail of blood
wherever he goes, a kind of Golem, in effect, who
has been planted in the world and operated as a lethal
weapon of divine will.[18]

But, suddenly, a riddle. Clever, subtle, lyrical.

He could have entertained his guests with a
demonstration of the power of his enormous muscles.
Or executed some amazing physical stunt, nothing
dangerous, like collapsing the pillars that supported
the building, but definitely a feat that would have
left them open-mouthed.

But instead he poses a riddle. And no ordinary
riddle, but rather one that he knows there is no
chance of them solving: for this is not a riddle whose
solution is based on something they already know,
or a puzzle of logic that they can think through.
Which means that he asks them a riddle that, as far
as they are concerned, has no solution.

Three, five, seven days they get caught up more
and more in the trap he has set for them. The party

goes on, but the atmosphere grows foul. There is a
mystery in the air and little by little it becomes
greater than the riddle itself, until the attention of
the reader cannot fail to turn from the riddle to the
one who asked it, and his motives.

For seven full days Samson circulates among his
guests, toys with their unknowingness, their curiosity,
their mounting anger. Now and then he listens to their
clumsy attempts to solve the riddle and shakes his head
again and again, politely, with mild mockery and undis-
guised pleasure. Owing to the Nazirite prohibition, he
does not drink the wine served to the guests. They of
course do not refrain from drinking, but rather try to
drown their frustration and rage, and Samson's absten-
tion from the collective boozing only intensifies their
antipathy toward him. In short, one can assume that
within the first day or two the Philistines were fed up
with the riddle, and surely from the outset had no
intention of plumbing the depths of this bizarre
stranger's soul. The whole situation infuriates them –
not least the thirty linen garments and sets of clothing they will have to pay him.

'Out of the eater came something to eat/ Out of the strong came something sweet.'

It would seem that that there are few things that can make a person crazier than the unabating abuse of an unanswerable riddle. (The case of Samson's riddle is probably the only place in the Bible where even a consummate Jewish patriot can identify greatly with the Philistines.) And as for Samson, one can truly feel how he secretly derives profound pleasure from what is happening. From their inability to solve the riddle, and from the intimate, quasi-erotic friction – as perceived by the riddler – between those who seek the answer and the elusive answer itself.

And perhaps –

Perhaps he asks them an impossible riddle like this precisely because a man who lives his whole life with a big riddle inside – a mystery that he too cannot solve – feels a great compulsion to create puzzlement in any way possible? For after three, five, seven days like these, the riddle-maker himself turns into a riddle, into a large vessel containing a bubbling secret, straining to explode . . .

And maybe this is what motivates Samson, and not only in this instance. He goes through life like a walking enigma, marvelling over his secret, his riddle. He enjoys approaching the dangerous brink of being found out by others. Yet, on second thoughts, the word 'enjoys' is inaccurate: more likely he is *driven* to this, compelled to confront this feeling, this bitter-tasting knowledge that he is impenetrable, that he cannot be released from his strangeness, nor from the mystery within.

On the seventh day the companions are sick and tired of the whole thing. In no uncertain terms they say to Samson's wife: 'Coax your husband to provide us with the answer to the riddle; else we shall put you and your father's household to the fire.'

'During the seven days of the feast,' reads the text, 'she continued to harass him with her tears.'

In other words, on top of the 'companions'' grow-ing rage, Samson all week long has endured an earful of his wife's weeping! For seven days she has been crying and pestering him to tell her the answer, and he keeps silent. This woman, who pleased him to the point that he ignored his parents' entreaties not to marry her – suddenly he is prepared to cause her such anguish, indeed to abuse her.

But why? Is it because he is trying to tell her, this first woman in his life, that even she will never know him fully? Or perhaps these seven days are a kind of exhausting initiation rite that he has set up for himself, a private ceremony of boundary definition, setting the limits of his willingness to allow another person, even a loved one, to enter the *sanctum sanctorum* of his soul, the place where his secret is hidden?

'You really hate me, you don't love me,' she wails bitterly. 'You asked my countrymen a riddle, and you didn't tell me the answer . . .'

And for a moment, on reading her words, it seems that in the complaint of the young bride there is a faint echo of something much broader and more complicated than a family quarrel, a hint of a riddle many times greater and more complex: namely the conundrum of the Jewish people as perceived by the nations of the world from antiquity until our own time, the wonderment and suspicion that have accompanied – and still often accompany – the Jew in his contact with other people, and the aura of mystery, otherness, and isolation that surrounds him, in their view. But let us leave such deep reflections aside and return to the young man and woman, to their first spat, which goes on for a whole week and is soaked in tears and nagging and stubborn refusal, until in the end the husband runs out of patience and snaps at his wife: 'I haven't even told my mother and father, and I should tell you?'

And the narrator perhaps did Samson a favour by not recording his wife's response.

'Hence a man leaves his father and mother and clings to his wife, so that they become one flesh,' says the Book of Genesis,[19] and indeed the very meaning of marriage is, among other things, that a man departs from his parents and chooses a woman to be his intimate partner. But from the sound of Samson's words one gathers that, for him, the matter is not so clear-cut, and there is a certain looseness and ambiguity in the practical implementation of leaving the parents and becoming 'one flesh'. 'If I haven't revealed the secret to my parents' – he says, in effect, to the woman he has just married – 'then it goes without saying that I won't tell you!' In other words, in the midst of his wedding feast, Samson declares with heavy-handed childishness, with rather infantile condescension, that his parents still take priority for him in all that concerns closeness and intimacy.

But in the end, after all her nagging, or maybe because of the very ordinary human temptation to boast a bit to his wife, Samson's resolve falters and he tells her the answer. The text doesn't say exactly what he tells her, nor, more importantly, *how* he tells her: does he show off as he describes his fight with the lion? Or is he modest? And does he convey only the dry facts, or in the heat of storytelling does he add a few colourful details, describing, for example, the extraordinary sight – the honey glistening amid the lion's sun-bleached ribs, the buzzing swarm of bees . . .

And if he in fact tells her everything, what

happened to him during the fight and how he felt afterwards, as he stood before the carcass, and the taste of the honey and the humming of the bees, is he telling her this in the hope of igniting a new spark of attraction? Does he hope she will understand what his parents did not?

And what happens next? Does she look at him with astonishment, with wonder? With confusion, or maybe revulsion? And maybe a new, wild arousal toward this man of hers, whom she suddenly realises is far more than he seems? Does she sense that with these words he is handing over something extra, not only the answer to this particular riddle, but also a clue to the solution to the riddle that is *him*?

And if so many questions pile up here, it's because this is, after all, a fateful moment for Samson: even if he only gave her the barest hint of what lies behind the riddle, this is the first time he has exposed something of his miraculous, hidden side to anyone, and has spoken of the event that he had not even revealed to his parents.

But the woman, torn every which way by simultaneous pressures both internal and external, is not equal to the task of secret-sharer. Scared to death of her countrymen, she tells them the answer.

Let us, for a moment, wishfully consider the possibility that this woman, whose name we do not even know, was in fact worthy of the trust Samson placed in her. What would have happened next, and what might Samson's life have looked like later on, if she had been able to look straight into him, to see him as he really was? To fathom what had befallen this foreigner even before he was born: a state of eternal non-belonging. To see a man who tears a lion apart with his bare hands and then melts before the sheer poetry of the honey in its carcass. To embrace the miraculous possibility that his greatest wish is that one person love him simply, wholly, naturally, not because of his miraculous quality, but in spite of it.

And although it is not stated explicitly that Samson loved this woman, what is written about her was apparently very important to Samson: she looked 'right' to him. *Yesharah*, reads the Hebrew, twice, from the word meaning 'straight' or 'honest'. In other words, there was something in her that seemed honest to him. And if so, she seemed like a person who was free of the innuendo and duplicity he had encountered from others throughout his life. This 'straightness' of hers promised him the possibility of peace of mind, of tranquillity. From the way she looked at him he got the feeling that he was at last accepted for what he was, and quite likely it was mainly because of this that the woman from Timnah was the one he first chose.

Yet she too betrayed him, immediately. In fact, he could have foreseen it. From the first he should never have pushed her into the bind of dual loyalty – to him and to her people. Nonetheless, this is exactly what he did, and in effect clear-headedly 'invited' her betrayal, condemned her to betray him. And thus arises the troubling suspicion that this is just what he wanted.[20]

'What is sweeter than honey', the Philistines answer him, 'and what is stronger than a lion?' Those who answer now are not only the 'companions' but 'the townsmen'. In other words, not only has his intimate secret been revealed, but it has spread beyond the wedding feast to the whole town of Timnah and become common knowledge among its residents. Samson steams with fury: 'Had you not ploughed with my heifer, you would not have guessed my riddle!' he roars, hurling an accusation thick with sexual overtones. (Though even in his fury he manages to wax poetic.) He is enraged, of course, filled with natural human anger, at the companions who managed, in the end, to outfox him; but what burns him more is his wife's disloyalty, since for the first time in his life he had dared to bring someone else close to an interior place which had previously belonged to him alone, a place of sweetness inside the raw power, and it was there, of all places, that he was betrayed.

For no sooner had he told her his secret, and perhaps attained a rare moment of confessional grace, than their intimate space was suddenly filled with total strangers. One can only imagine the intense pain that overcame Samson, that penetrated the nameless, inarticulate core of his being, down into a primal, intimate moment, when the 'meeting-place' of mother and foetus had been invaded by a stranger.

But there is, perhaps, another possible reason for this terrible fury, which will fuel his future acts of revenge and mass murder.

Let us try to imagine the conversation between his wife and the companions: according to the biblical text, she came and 'explained the riddle to her countrymen'. But did she reveal to them a bit more than that? Did she also tell them about the deeper truth she had just discovered about Samson? It is of course difficult to tell if she herself had grasped the full significance of the revelation granted her by Samson. Something in the wording of the Philistines' answer to Samson gives the impression that, even after hearing what she said, they still don't know much. Not about Samson, nor about the major event hinted at by his riddle. It would seem that they got from his wife only an essential synopsis of what happened, something about a dead lion and honey, and with what little they have, they challenge him and pretend they know more than they actually do.

This is only conjecture. But if there is anything to it, this raises the possibility that it was the very brevity of the Philistines' answer, their too-clever, laconic response, that more than anything ignited Samson's wrath.

For it is likely that when he hears the words 'What is sweeter than honey and what is stronger than a lion?' from their lips, Samson senses that the secret he holds so dear, the secret that expresses his uniqueness, his chosenness, has been sullied and diminished, turned almost into a joke, into something that can be distilled into a glib one-liner that sounds like a jingle; instantly transforming a treasure into worn-out currency, cheap gossip that any 'townsman' can pass along to his pals, even if he doesn't actually understand what is concealed within it.

In his *Letters to a Young Poet*, Rainer Maria Rilke wrote: 'And those who live the mystery falsely and badly (and they are very many), lose it only for themselves and nevertheless pass it on like a sealed letter, without knowing it.' [21]

These profound words, read against Samson's life, illuminate it in ways that alternate between irony and pathos: Samson himself contains a secret, a *mystery*, but he also often 'lives that mystery badly' (as in the case of the harlot from Gaza, whom we will meet anon). He himself acts sometimes like one who has been sentenced to pass along the mystery 'like a sealed letter', that is to say, to carry out the divine plan that chose him, without his understanding it fully, a mystery moulded inside him from the womb.

Either way, one thing is certain: that a person will always, always feel deeply humiliated when his secret is tossed about among strangers who do not understand, who are unworthy. This is what Samson was sure to feel when he heard the answer to his riddle from the 'companions', rejoicing in his distress. And since we are speaking of Samson, it may be added that this was, perhaps, the feeling of an artist whose life's work has been displayed in public and has received a blank reaction, devoid of understanding, and even derisive.

Burning with anger and humiliation he goes down to Ashkelon, the Philistine city, and there kills thirty men.

One wonders why Samson went all the way to Ashkelon, a distance of some forty kilometres, instead of, say, to the Philistine city of Ekron, a mere five kilometres from Timnah. Why did he prefer to travel dozens of kilometres in Philistine territory? And maybe the answer is contained within the question, and Samson felt a need to penetrate as deep as he could into Philistine existence, to rub up more and more against the foreigners, the mockers, the haters?

He cuts down thirty innocent people, who had the bad luck to run into him in the streets of their city. He steals their clothes and brings them to the thirty companions. Just as they had cut him to the quick, he does the same to thirty strangers. He slays them and 'skins' them, in effect – a thoroughly vile act that attests, in its way, to Samson's tendency to confuse, in a frightening manner, exterior and essence, the secret and the strange.

Following the collapse of his marriage, and the blow dealt him by the world, Samson returns, like a child, to the house of his mother and father. And let us remember: he has married, he has left his parents' home – and he returns yet again, to lick his wounds, to be consoled a bit at the parental hearth. But before long, at the time of the wheat harvest, he goes back to Timnah. Again the umbilical cord is stretched, again he attempts to separate from his parents and return to his Philistine wife.

Clasped to his breast he carries a baby goat, a peace offering, and attempts to visit the woman, but this turns out to be impossible: her father has already given her to another man: a 'companion', apparently one of the *mere'im* from the wedding feast, the very men who had forced his wife to reveal his secret. Her father offers Samson, as was the custom in those days, her younger sister, who is, in his words, 'more beautiful than she', but Samson is already smouldering with anger: 'Now the Philistines can have no claim against me for the harm I shall do them,' he says, and goes off to exact his revenge.

★   ★   ★

'Samson went and caught three hundred foxes. He took torches and, turning the foxes tail to tail, he placed a torch between each pair of tails. He lit the torches and turned the foxes loose among the standing grain of the Philistines, setting fire to stacked grain, standing grain, vineyards, and olive trees.'

This act of Samson's is also terribly barbaric and cruel. But what grand, well-crafted, indeed aesthetic revenge it is!

Just think what kind of effort a man must invest in order to catch three hundred foxes, tie them in pairs to one another, tie torches between them and then light them, and then send them out into the fields.

But no less impressive than the physical under-taking are the planning, the idea, the inventiveness. The Bible, of course, abounds in grossly violent and brutal acts. (It would be interesting to compile a full catalogue of the types of mayhem and revenge that were commonplace in those days among Israel and its enemies, from the dismemberment of corpses and the slaughter of hundreds with a cattle prod, to the massive harvest of foreskins.) In contrast to all these, Samson takes a most original revenge that includes a manifestly artistic dimension. (In the language of modern art we would say that Samson's exploit of the burning foxes constitutes a *performance*.) This is a demonstration not only of the man's physical strength, but also of his style, which will continue to be stamped upon all his deeds, large and small, upon his every gesture and contact with the world.

But if indeed there is, in Samson, something of the artist, this is significant not only for the content of his expression but also its form: a feat like this is hardly the product of mere whim. Much thought has been invested, with a precise intention in mind: Samson, after all, could have tied a torch to the tail of each individual fox, and dispatched it to set fire to the stacked and standing grain, and thus dealt the Philistines a far heavier blow! But such a deed, apparently, would not have satisfied his deep impulse, his 'artistic' need to draw upon something private and singular in everything he does.

Let us again read the story he's telling us here, written in letters of foxes and fire. He ties the foxes in pairs. He fixes a flaming torch between them. We can feel what happens to the foxes at this moment, the crazed running as they try to break free of the other fox, their twin, whom they think is the one that is burning them. All of a sudden each is transformed into a dual being, all afire, that cannot be saved from itself. Each fox tries to escape in a different direction but drags his double, his opposite, his nemesis, along with him.

This is apparently what bursts from the depths of Samson's soul as his hidden 'artistic signature', which he heaves with all his strength at the world. His doubleness, the fire raging within him, the powerful urges that tear him to shreds, the pairs of conflicting forces warring inside him always:

monasticism and lust, the super-muscled frame and artistic-spiritual heart; the murderous cruelty that erupts from him, versus the poet within; the recognition that he may only be the tool of a 'divine providence' that utilises him as it sees fit, alongside powerful flickerings of free will and the urge for personal expression. On top of which is his determination to keep his secret to himself, together with the blatant and desperate need to reveal himself to one other intimate soul.

Is it any wonder that he requires no fewer than three hundred foxes to express all this?

The foxes, living torches, run around in the fields, sowing fiery devastation, destroying all the gathered crops (this was, recall, 'the season of the wheat harvest'), and they also die in the process, as a prophecy of sorts thrown out by Samson, though he cannot now interpret it: 'Let me die with the Philistines.'

\*   \*   \*

The Philistines take revenge upon the person whom they believe brought this disaster upon them, namely the woman from Timnah. They go there and burn her and her father. Fire for fire. Samson pays them back and 'smote them leg as well as thigh, a great smiting'. Thus from one minute to the next this strange war of one man against a whole nation becomes increasingly problematic. For here is a man destined from his mother's womb 'to deliver Israel', but it turns out that this 'deliverance' never deviates from the massive destruction of Philistines.

Here it is essential to recall what may have been forgotten in the heat of the narrative: that Samson was a *Judge*. A national leader who judged his people for twenty years. A strange judge, to be sure: when did he have the slightest contact with his own people? When did he deal with their issues or sit to adjudicate between them? After all, as anyone who has read the story knows, Samson's life and works are always directed outside, toward the Philistines, with whom he falls in love and shares a banquet table, upon whom he takes revenge and makes war (and thus he often seems to the reader to be a character more 'Philistine' than Jewish).

Nevertheless, his tale earned a place in the Bible, where it is told at length and in detail; and if at times the Jewish tradition has read Samson pejoratively – owing to his aggressiveness, his roguish behaviour and skirt-chasing – he is also inscribed in the Jewish consciousness as a national hero and a symbol. Perhaps this is because, despite everything, in the deep structures of his personality – his loneliness and isolation, his strong need to preserve his separateness and mystery, yet also his limitless desire to mix and assimilate with gentiles – Samson expresses and implies qualities that are 'Jewish' indeed.

And this too, of course: Jews throughout the ages took pride in the tales of his heroism and yearned for the physical strength, bravery, and manliness that he represented. They esteemed, no less, his ability to apply force without any restraints or moral inhibitions, an ability which history withheld from the trod-upon Jews for millennia, until the establishment of the State of Israel.

In Hebrew, he is almost always referred to as 'Samson the hero', and elite combat units of the Israeli army have been named after him, from 'Samson's Foxes' of the 1948 War of Independence to the 'Samson' unit created during the first Palestinian *intifada* in the late 1980s (not to mention a chain of body-building clubs called the 'Samson Institute', set up in the 1960s, by a muscle-bound rabbi named Rafael Halperin).

Yet there is a certain problematic quality to Israeli sovereignty that is also embodied in Samson's relationship to his own power. As in the case of Samson, it sometimes seems that Israel's considerable military might is an asset that becomes a liability. For it would seem, without taking lightly the dangers facing Israel, that the reality of being immensely powerful has not really been internalised in the Israeli consciousness, not assimilated in a natural way, over many generations; and this, perhaps, is why the attitude to this power, whose acquisition has often been regarded as truly miraculous, is prone to distortion.

Such distortion may lead, for example, to ascribing an exaggerated value to the power that one has attained; to making power an end in itself; and to using it excessively; and also to a tendency to turn almost automatically to the use of force instead of weighing other means of action – these are all, in the end, characteristically 'Samsonian' modes of behaviour.

To this may be added the well-known Israeli feeling, in the face of any threat that comes along, that the country's security is crumbling – a feeling that also exists in the case of Samson, who in certain situations seems to shatter into pieces, his strength vanishing in the blink of an eye. This kind of collapse, however, does not reflect one's actual strength, and often carries in its wake an overblown display of force, further complicating the situation. All of this attests, it would seem, to a rather feeble sense of ownership of the power that has been attained, and, of course, to a deep existential insecurity. This is connected, without a doubt, to the very real dangers lying in wait for Israel, but also

to the tragic formative experience of being a
stranger in the world, the Jewish sense of not being
a nation 'like other nations', and of the State of
Israel as a country whose very existence is condi-
tional, whose future is in doubt and steeped in jeop-
ardy, feelings that all the nuclear bombs that Israel
developed, in a program once known as the 'Samson
Option', cannot eradicate.

★   ★   ★

After smiting the Philistines, Samson goes and
establishes residence in the cave of the rock of
Etam, which would appear to be located near the
town of Etam in the territory of the tribe of
Judah.[22] There he sits by himself, in apparent retire-
ment from society after being disappointed in
mankind.

Except that now the Philistines get ready to take
their revenge. They head for Judah and prepare
themselves for battle. The men of Judah, frightened by the Philistine mobilisation, come to ask

why on earth the Philistines are preparing to make war upon them, and the Philistines explain: 'We have come to take Samson prisoner, and to do to him as he did to us.'

Three thousand men of Judah proceed apace to Samson's dwelling place in the cave of the rock of Etam. Samson, it will be recalled, is not a member of the tribe of Judah, and he is about to bring down upon them a war that does not 'belong' to them. 'You knew that the Philistines rule over us', they say to him anxiously, 'why have you done this to us?' Three thousand men stand around him filled with trepidation, and Samson, with simple, stubborn logic, replies: 'As they did to me, so I did to them.'

Three thousand men steal glances at one another. One can almost hear the uneasy throat-clearing. 'We have come down to take you prisoner', they finally dare to tell him, 'and to hand you over to the Philistines.' And across the gulf of centuries one can sense the plea gurgling in their voices: Don't make it harder for us, just come quietly and we'll finish this filthy business in a dignified fashion . . .

This episode is one that's easy to skip past in the Samson story, since it doesn't stand out amid the other dramatic events that are painted in such bold colours. But we, who read Samson's story with keen interest in the frequent shifts he makes among friend, foreigner, and foe; we, who sense how Samson is fated over and over to agonise over the riddle of his strangeness in relation to his parents (and his people, and in fact the whole human race); we will dwell a while on this brief passage.

They stand before him bewildered. They are astounded by the extreme loneliness that radiates from this man who has nested in a rock. A man whose boldness may already be legendary among the tribes of Israel, but who also evokes fear and anger because of his repeated provocations of the vengeful Philistines. And not only fear and anger does he bring out in these men: for he, alone, dares to do what they, in their multitudes, do not dare do. And maybe somewhere in their hearts, in a tiny corner that remains free, not enslaved or exhausted from the weight of Philistine conquest, they can guess that one day, in the annals of their people, it will be Samson – not they – who will be the symbol of resistance to occupation and tyranny.

We have come to take you prisoner, they mumble, to hand you over to the Philistines . . . there is almost no doubt that at this moment they hate Samson no less than they despise the Philistines. Were they not terrified of him, they would surely overrun him themselves and do the Philistines' work for them. And here, amazingly enough, Samson doesn't even argue with them. Only this does he ask of them: 'Swear to me that you yourselves will not attack me.' And they indeed promise not to hurt him, only to take him prisoner and turn him over to the Philistines; 'we will not slay you.'

The exchange between Samson and the men of Judah is described rather gently, even compassionately. Something in the conversation almost tugs at the reader's sleeve and implores him or her to pay attention to what is going on: the men of Judah are careful not to harm Samson. Even as they are

DAVID GROSSMAN

furious with him, they take pains to maintain a respectful, even worshipful, distance. The reader, who has already caught a glimpse of Samson's inner life, knows that he is likely to experience this distance not only as a sign of respect but also as an expression of estrangement and avoidance. Samson knows well this attitude towards him, the degree of respect, the awe that pushes him again, as always, into loneliness and isolation.

It will be recalled that these are his own people who are doing this to him. Members of his people, whose judge – whose leader – he is. It never occurs to them to object, even in a token manner, to the Philistines' demands and to risk their lives for him. Nor do they offer, for example, to arrange his escape from their territory and find ways to placate the Philistines. They want to hand him over, and do not conceal their eagerness to be rid of the ongoing danger that he embodies. And he is doubtless aware of this, of their motives and their enthusiasm, but does not come to them with complaints: 'Swear to me that you yourselves will not attack me' – no more than this does he ask of them at this critical moment. For he knows that they cannot kill him, that he is stronger than all of them combined, but he apparently has a touching, almost pathetic need to hear from them – from their very lips – this soothing, protective promise, these exact words, 'we will not slay you'. As if with these words they, his brothers, can lighten the eternal burden forced upon him by his mother, when she announced his death even before he was born.

They tie him up with two new ropes. Those who have read the entire Samson story will recall that when Delilah asks him, later on, how he can be tied up and made helpless he mocks her and says 'new ropes'; and when she ties him up he snaps them off his arms like thread.

But here he allows the men of Judah to tie him with the same kind of ropes. He stands among them, perhaps taller than them all, permits them to wrap him in their web, feels the bonds of betrayal tightening around his flesh, lets them hand him over to the foreigners.

And this passivity raises the impression that Samson is almost enjoying this, taking strange, bitter, convoluted pleasure from the whole affair. As if he were taking part in an utterly private ritual, in which the men of Judah are mere puppets on a string; and what manipulates these strings are Samson's deepest, most elemental needs, the need to relive, again and again, the experience of being betrayed by those close to him, the compulsion to re-enact, over and over, that primal event of being handed over to strangers, of being given up.

And then, after draining from the encounter with his countrymen every drop of that foul nectar that apparently fuels his soul, he reverts to his familiar acts of force and violence: It occurs when the men of Judah take him away from the rock, and lead him to the Philistines who stand in formation at a place called 'Lehi', which in Hebrew means 'cheek' or 'jaw'.

Even someone who wasn't there can conjure in his mind the sight of three thousand men of Judah in a long Lilliputian parade, carrying Samson, bound by ropes, like a giant statue. When the Philistines see him they cheer wildly, victoriously, but when they go to seize him, the spirit of God once again comes over Samson. His body is so inflamed with the passion for revenge that the ropes around his arms disintegrate 'like flax that catches fire'. He reaches out and finds, just by chance, the fresh jawbone of an ass, with which he smites a thousand Philistines.

When he finishes the job, again the poet bursts from the bully: 'With the jaw of an ass', he declaims, 'Mass upon mass!/ With the jaw of an ass/ I have slain a thousand men.' And we too, amid the horrific slaughter, find enough poetry within ourselves to remark that this 'trademark' mode of expression, and Samson's creativity and ingenuity, are enshrined in the very weapons he uses – foxes, an ass's jawbone, bare hands against a lion, exclusively 'organic' materials, natural and original.

He is very thirsty 'as he finished speaking' (and it is not entirely clear whether this is from the exertion of wiping out a thousand men, or from composing his little poem). He calls out to God, 'You yourself have granted this great victory through Your servant; and must I now die of thirst and fall into the hands of the uncircumcised?' And this cry pierces the heart, because Samson is so weak and vulnerable here: he almost sounds like a boy sobbing to his father, and also like someone achingly despondent over the failure of the 'grand plan' that he never presumes fully to understand, knowing only that he serves it as a vessel or an instrument.

Let us tarry a bit longer over this last outburst of his, and again contemplate his sudden, sharp transition from superhero and mass murderer to a near-child: in the blink of an eye, and with astonishing ease, it's as if the warrior's spine has snapped, and he crumbles, crying desperately for the embrace of a caring, compassionate parent.

Samson's cry is also surprising because, for an instant, there is a parting of the curtain and it turns out that Samson speaks directly to God. Speech like this attests, of course, to a special relationship with multiple implications, nothing of which has been heretofore vouchsafed by the biblical storyteller. And even if it will in no way alter Samson's well-known destiny, this revelation is a bit comforting, as it lessens somewhat his isolation among his brethren, among his fellow man.

But it may well be that within Samson's plea lies another, very human, drama, having to do with his relationship with God: perhaps Samson understands that the affliction of thirst is a divine punishment for the arrogance he exhibited in his victory speech by suggesting that it was he alone, he and the jawbone of an ass – without God's help – who slew the Philistines. Now, on his hands and knees on the rock, fainting from thirst, Samson promises his God that he knows well who brought about the victory: 'You yourself have granted this great victory through Your servant,' he gasps, and God accepts the 'thank-you' that includes regret and apology, and splits open 'the hollow which is at Lehi', and water gushes from it.

\*   \*   \*

And after all this – 'Samson went to Gaza, where he
met a whore and slept with her.'

There are, as is widely known, various reasons
why a man goes to a prostitute; but before we spec-
ulate about Samson's motives, and even before we
remind ourselves that he is a Nazirite (for in
Samson's case it's easy to forget this, since he is one
of those Nazirites who is not forbidden contact with
women) – perhaps we should ask why he went to
Gaza at all? Why to this Philistine city, of all places,
whose residents surely want him dead?

How to make sense of Samson's bizarre compulsion to mingle with Philistines? To mingle his flesh
with theirs, to mangle them with his fists: indeed
all his contact with them is tangled up with the
body, flesh and fluid, wrestling and writhing, pierc-
ing and penetrating. Those inclined to do so can infer
here, among other things, a dimly perceived wish on
Samson's part that his intensive contact with others,

especially foreigners, will grant him something that may be missing from the root of his being: a feeling of actual, physical existence and of its tried and true boundaries.

For nowhere in Samson's universe is there a single person who resembles him even a little. In this sense, Samson lives and functions in a vacuum. Within this void materialises his identity – elusive, defying definition, filled with contradictions, legendary, miraculous. It is not hard to imagine the confusion that reigns in such a soul, which is in constant need of 'signals' from the outside world and other people in order to define its limits. Small wonder, then, that a man like this is drawn again and again to rub up against another being that is utterly foreign and at first glance seems to inhabit a sharply defined, almost one-dimensional space. When he is in contact with this other being he can feel – apart from satisfaction over fulfilling his divine mission – its boundary, the fence that separates him from it, and thus he can feel his own limit and maybe even his definition. And therefore, it is to Gaza that he goes, to the Philistine city, to be among foreigners, others, the different ones, to brush up against them, to tangle and wriggle with them, to kill and love them and then kill them again . . .

And another notion arises, that maybe Samson has an inner need to divide up his existence among people and places that are very different and removed from one another. That is, to compartmentalise, to spread himself around as much as possible, in order to protect the secret that is the heart and focus of his life. And therefore, out of a survival instinct of sorts, Samson must always be in motion, staying only a short while in any one place – Zorah, Eshtaol, Timnah, Ashkelon, Judah, Hebron, Nahal Sorek – and leaving abruptly, revealing a little bit and concealing more, thus creating a reality in which people everywhere will know only 'a part of Samson', only one piece of the mosaic, and maybe this will make it harder for them – the strangers who only catch a glimpse of him – to understand the whole picture and to unravel, once and for all, the riddle of Samson.

(And as one reads the descriptions of Samson's motion, frequent, forceful and slightly mad, one may get a flash of his mother striding briskly through the fields, on her way to tell Manoah about her meeting with the angel. 'The woman ran in haste,' reads the text, and it's as if she imprinted upon the embryo within her the power, the momentum, and the sheer pleasure of that fast running . . .)

If Samson's trip to Gaza seems curious, his visit to the prostitute seems easier to explain. Samson is alone at the moment. He has no wife. When we recall that, as soon as he became energised by the divine spirit, he went off to seek love, we can only imagine the depth of his loneliness and anguish now, in the aftermath of his sojourn in the cave of the rock of Etam. But it is certainly also possible that Samson goes to the whore because of the bitter disappointment of his previous – and sole – experience with a woman, his wife, the girl from Timnah who was given to another. And if so, with all due respect to Samson's robust sexual urges, his turning to a prostitute also signifies a loss of hope in

finding true love and in the possibility of entrust-
ing his secret, the keys to his soul, to another person
worthy of trust.

Furthermore, contact with a prostitute means
giving something precious and very personal to a
total stranger, to someone who has no real interest
in the essence of the person she or he is having sex
with. This is the off-putting element of prostitution,
and also, of course, the key to its appeal: the radi-
cal intersection of the most intimate and most impersonal, the most private and the utterly public, the
sperm and the stranger.

Viewed this way, it is clear why Samson would
choose this option: when he sleeps with a whore,
he again exposes his 'mystery' to a complete
stranger. Again he flirts with that need he has, to
give without giving himself away, to pose a riddle
but withhold the solution. Yet again he can be in
the midst of the most intimate act, the act of *knowing*, and remain unknown, undeciphered.

For this would appear to be what Samson is always
looking for — that point of elusive, dubious contact

that never offers full satisfaction, or solace, or genuine closeness. And least of all, love. Which never provides what he needs most – to be given fully to another, and to be received by that person in a way that enables full self-disclosure, so that, perhaps, he may be healed at last of the remoteness he has felt since birth.

Why does he behave this way? Why does he never try to redeem himself with the help of another 'appropriate' soul, who might be truly responsive to his deep need, and cure him of his dreadful core experience of strangeness?

We can broaden the question to inquire why, so frequently, do people undermine themselves in the very areas where they need the greatest salvation? This is the case for individuals, yet also for societies and nations, which so often seem fated to repeat, with depressing regularity, the most tragic choices and decisions of their history. And in Samson's case, too, this destructive force is definitely at work, which is apparently why he manages all his life to be true to the distortions imposed on him by others, and is again and again alienated from his own vital and authentic needs – the need for genuine love and acceptance, the yearning for relationships of honesty and trust.

Which is why Samson goes not only to a whore but to a whore from Gaza. In other words, to a place doubly alien, and moreover to a woman who he is sure will immediately turn him over to her countrymen; in any case a visit that will surely lead to his falling into the hands of the Philistines, who for quite some time have been raring to take revenge for everything he has done to them.

And indeed when the Gazans learn that Samson is to be found at the house of the prostitute, they gather at once and lie in wait for him at the gates to the city, through which he will have to pass on his way out of town. They lie there in silence all night, intending to capture him at daybreak and kill him. But Samson stays with the woman only until the middle of the night; then he rises, goes to the city gate and surprises the ambushers. It would seem that he guessed the Philistines' plot and therefore left the whore earlier than expected in order to take them by surprise. And if so, this lends credence to the speculation that it wasn't just the whore he was after, but also the experience (and even the 'joy') of fear, tension, and humiliation bound up in the very act of making love to her – not merely because of her expected disloyalty, but also, perhaps mainly, from the knowledge that at the heart of their sexual intimacy, strangers are also present.

These strangers are in fact far away at this moment, but they are very much present in their intentions and in the air of conspiracy that spills into the room where the two are making love. And this way Samson gets to seize the two electrodes of feeling that he courts incessantly: powerful intimacy, together with the penetrating recognition that the borders of secrecy and privacy surrounding him and the woman are open to one and all, and that their sexual union has been violated from the first. This way he reconfirms to himself the recognition that has in large degree shaped his life and determined his path, and will continue to make him miserable till his last day, namely, that intimacy – all intimacy – is, by definition, polluted.

'At midnight he got up, grasped the doors of the town gate together with the two gateposts, and pulled them out along with the bar. He placed them on his shoulders and carried them off to the top of the hill that is near to Hebron.'

And though, as we noted, it is never said that Samson was a giant, here he seems gargantuan. As he does in the famous illustration by Gustave Doré, 'Samson Carrying Away the Gates of Gaza', in which Samson is seen climbing a hill (apparently approaching Hebron; there are no such hills in the Gaza area).[23] The sky above him seems to open, and he is showered with celestial radiance. But Samson himself does not see this light; he nearly collapses under the weight of the huge gate, which separates him from the light, and the image is one of a being who is half-godly and half-human, suffering and afflicted.

Here too, as in all of Samson's exploits, is a feat the like of which is nowhere else to be found in the

Bible, and which again is a kind of extravagant, significant performance: a stranger comes to the city, and when he leaves he takes with him its gates, the very thing that divides the inside from the outside. He penetrates the boundary of the city and confiscates the barrier that creates the distinction between the locals and outsiders or enemies. This too, of course, carries a symbolism that is anything but foreign to Samson's internal discourse, but here it is framed from a new angle: in the uprooting of the gates can be discerned not only Samson's familiar, even reflexive intention to hurt and humiliate the Philistines; but also, if you will, an echo of defiance, even a unique *protest* on Samson's part against the violation of his own intimacy.

And thus, from the sight of this man ripping out the gates and bearing them off on his back, the reader may derive mild comfort from the thought that, even if Samson's great mission of battling the Philistines has been imposed on him from above, and if his whole life is a journey determined in advance, here Samson manages to muster a few sparks of free will, as yet again he finds a uniquely self-expressive mode of carrying out his task.

★   ★   ★

In the woods, on the way to Tel Zorah – the mound that is believed to mark the spot of the biblical Zorah – can be found yellow signs pointing to the 'Grave of Samson and Manoah', an irresistible spur to curiosity. The mound, of greyish brown rendzina soil, is covered by an assortment of thorns and sparse yellow stubble. At the crest is a patch of concrete and two graves, a modest tomb of sorts fashioned of stone blocks with a pair of little blue domes. On one of these is written, 'The Righteous Judge of Israel, Samson the Hero, of Blessed Memory, Who Judged Israel as Did Their Father in Heaven'. Also inscribed is the day of Samson's death: the 24th of Tammuz. 'The Righteous Manoah', it says, in the calligraphy used by scribes of Torah scrolls, on the other dome, 'of Blessed Memory, Who Saw an Angel of God Face to Face'. Incidentally, Samson's mother, whose encounters with the angel were closer than her husband's, merited neither a grave nor a monument in the family plot.

These, of course, are not the actual graves of Samson and his father. No one knows who, if anyone, is buried here. The monument suddenly appeared in the late 1990s, its provenance unclear. But the spot was quickly sanctified by believers, who come here, singly and in groups, lighting little oil lamps at the foot of the graves, praying for cure from illness, brides and grooms for their children, success in business, babies for their barren daughters. At midnight, one may find Hasidic Jews of the Bratzlaver sect who have come to pray for redemption and mourn the destruction of the Temple.

Nearby is the mouth of a large cave. The concave receptacles of an olive press are carved in the stone. Once a donkey walked here in an endless circle, turning a round millstone – which today lies here, broken – that pressed the oil from the olives. A large square wine-press is also carved out of the stone floor. From its size it would seem to have been one of the main wine-presses of the region, and since grapes needed to arrive at the press as soon as possible after being picked, one may gather that the terraces at the foot of Tel Zorah once teemed with grapevines.

At the top of the mound, beside the graves, someone has placed a tiny cupboard containing bibles and prayerbooks. One small bible, with bus tickets stuck in its pages as bookmarks, opens at once to a wrinkled, frequently fingered page, stained with sweat and tears:

'After that, he fell in love with a woman in Nahal Sorek, named Delilah.'

\*　\*　\*

Who is Delilah? The Bible furnishes no answer, not even whether she was a Philistine like Samson's other women. On the other hand, she is the first woman in the story who is identified by name, and the only one whom Samson explicitly loved. But where did he meet her? What did he see in her? There is no way of knowing. Nor how he courted her, and what was different this time, when he was actually in love, as opposed to the others. And most of all – what does the silence of the text suggest about the feelings of Delilah toward Samson?

The biblical narrator, as we have seen, is reluctant to impart this sort of information. He is more interested in actions here, just as when he rushed from 'the woman bore a son, and she named him Samson; the boy grew up, and the Lord blessed him' straight to 'the spirit of the Lord first moved him in the encampment of Dan, between Zorah and Eshtaol', skipping over Samson's childhood, purging the intriguing details about the education of this extraordinary child, about his childhood pleasures (Did he strangle snakes, like Hercules? Or battle a wild boar, like Odysseus?) and his friends, or rather, as we might expect, his utter loneliness. Nothing of this is known, and we are also unaware of any younger siblings, children born without any special mission, free of the burden of mystery, the ordinary children of ordinary parents.

And so too in the Delilah story – not a single detail offers a temporary pause in some cosy biographical nook in between the name of the new love and the forward momentum of the plot: 'The lords of the Philistines went up to her and said, "Coax him and find out what makes him so strong, and how we can overpower him, tie him up, and make him helpless; and we'll each give you eleven hundred shekels of silver."'

Various works dealing with the story of Samson – in literature, painting, music, film[24] – have tried to represent Delilah as a tragic figure, who had no intention of harming Samson and indeed was anguished over what happened to him after she turned him in. This sort of interpretation may be found, for example, in Van Dyck's painting *The Arrest of Samson*, in which Samson casts a heart-rending look at Delilah as the Philistines burst into the room, seize him and tear him away from her: Delilah's face is turned toward him in a curious mixture of satisfaction over her success, yet pain and tenderness too. Her hand is extended toward his face in a gesture that at the same time suggests a wave of farewell, of renunciation, but also a gesture of compassion, a yearning to caress him one last time, a tender send-off as he embarks on a road of suffering.

But the text as it stands does not lend itself to such a generous reading of Delilah's deeds and character, indeed rejects it outright. Delilah's entire behaviour does not even hint of love, and yet it is this cruel, treacherous woman whom Samson loves, and, as we have remarked, it may well be that note of treachery that he loves in her,[25] which forces the reader to broaden and loosen the very definition of love: it is probably Delilah's cruelty, her almost transparent passion to hurt him – a level of passion that he never found in his other women – which ties him to her with twisted bonds that turn out to be stronger than any that preceded them, and which therefore, for the first time, arouse his love.

But the explanation of the compulsive need for betrayal is, in the end, so depressing, constraining, mechanical – and denying of Samson's free will – that we seek, alongside it, another explanation, or wait a while and hope that the story itself will lead us to it.

Delilah – motivated by the promise of a handsome payoff by the Philistines – ties Samson up and teases him with a sort of two-faced foreplay. On the surface, she is trying to determine, with Samson's compliance, the secret to his strength and a means of binding him from which he cannot get himself free: 'If I were to be tied with seven fresh bowstrings that were never dried, 'I should become as weak as an ordinary man,' Samson answers, stretched out to his full length on the mattress, maybe idly stroking his long braids – all seven of them – and suppressing a smile.

Erotic amusements are a matter of taste, and being tied up with fresh tendons that have not been dried is apparently something Samson is into. Delilah at once passes the word about Samson's fancy to the Philistine officers. They send the requested accoutrements up to her chamber, and she ties the damp cords around his body. And all the while, remember, 'an ambush was waiting in her room', a most glaring example of the confusion and boundary-violation that always attend Samson's activities, indiscriminately mixing the intimate and the public, love and betrayal.

Delilah finishes wrapping his body with the cords, and then, when he is tied tight, she says to him (in a sudden cry? a confidential whisper in his ear?) 'Samson, the Philistines are upon you!' Barely a moment passes, and Samson pops the tendons apart as easily as a 'strand of tow' (i.e., a fibre of flax) comes apart at a mere 'touch of fire'.

You deceived me, declares Delilah, and lied to me. With astonishing coldness, and even as she spins her web of deceit, she accuses him of lying. Her eyes are perhaps flashing toward the 'ambusher', then fixing on Samson: 'Now, tell me true, how can you be tied up and restrained?'

Samson – sprawled on his back? stretching with satisfaction? – suggests a new method: 'If I were to be bound with new ropes that had never been used, I would become as frail as an ordinary man.'

*Haliti* is the word he uses – literally, 'I would
become ill' – which the medieval commentator Radak
reads more moderately as 'I would weaken.'

Delilah wastes no time. She takes new ropes, thick
and rough, ties him up and says again, 'Samson, the
Philistines are upon you!' The ambusher is poised to
attack, but Samson casually snaps these ropes too,
as if they were threads.

You deceived me, Delilah says again, you told me
lies. How can you be tied up? Samson obviously
realises that she is stubbornly repeating exactly what
she said before, signalling her unwillingness to give
up. 'If you weave the seven locks of my hair with
the warp-threads of a loom,' he says, 'then I will
surely weaken'. We can only guess at the gleam in
his eye and the timbre of his voice, but the words
he speaks reveal something new: until now he has
spoken to her in a different way. 'If I were to be
bound,' he has said – twice – in impersonal, general
terms, without specifying who would be doing the
binding, or might harm him. But here he turns to
her directly, with clear comprehension: 'If you

weave,' he tells her, if *you*, Delilah, weave the seven locks of my hair . . .

(And in the midst of this game that is not a game, and as sort of a momentary distraction from the terrible thing that will very soon happen, it is possible to muse over the fact that only now, towards the end of the story, is the reader informed that Samson had *seven* locks of hair. Something in this small new detail hints that Samson loved his hair, took good care of it, scrupulously separated and braided his tresses, lock by lock . . . And more: anyone who has grown very long hair knows how hard it is to take care of it on one's own; and here, a moment before these glorious locks will be shorn by a woman, our thoughts drift to a different woman, Samson's mother, who maybe helped him, during his childhood and youth, in braiding and combing and curling and washing – and perhaps did so even when he was grown up, in between his other women?)

Samson falls asleep. Maybe he was exhausted by the lovemaking, maybe he is starting to crack.

Delilah does not rest. She weaves his hair into a loom with a warp-thread and also pins it with a peg, to hold it firm, and says to him again, a third time, 'Samson, the Philistines are upon you', and Samson wakes up and in one motion pulls out the weave and the peg.

Thus, in what seemed at first like love-play but which gradually turns bitter, he surrenders himself to Delilah and her cords and ropes and tendons. And here it may be noted that Samson's whole life story is an endless braid of knots and ropes: foxes tied together, new ropes with which he is bound by the men of Judah, damp bowstrings and locks of hair woven into a loom, and time after time we see Samson's passion to tie and be tied, and also to be ensnared, and we may read this serpentine jumble of ropes – this tangled web – and wonder, how many ropes does a man need to replace one umbilical cord that was never properly spun?

Three times Delilah cries out, 'Samson, the Philistines are upon you', and each time, nonetheless, Samson suspends his suspicion of her machinations, and continues to cooperate in her transparent plot. Over and over he recognises that she is using his answers in an attempt to harm him, yet he does not protest or accuse her.[26]

But of course he is drawn not only to the treacherous Delilah but to the 'ambusher' who has been with them all along in the room, the stranger always hidden in the background, who in a certain sense needs to be there in order to complete, deep in Samson's soul, the primal scene of his life, the moment he was traumatised in the womb: mother, child, stranger.

And then, after Delilah has pestered and pressured him constantly – *va-tiktzar nafsho la-mut*, 'he was wearied to death'.

Nowhere else in the Bible does this phrase appear. The rabbis of antiquity found an original explanation for Samson's anguish, commenting that Delilah 'at the time of the consummation pulled away from under him'.[27] Arguably such a gross rejection might make a man lose his lust for life, yet all the same, the unique biblical wording calls for an alternative explanation, another motive for Samson's behaviour with Delilah.

For it is also possible to see it this way: that all of Delilah's banging on Samson's door, her unrelenting interrogation, 'What makes you so strong? And how could you be tied up and made helpless?' – in other words, what's your secret, who are you really, what kind of *man* are you inside that mystery and what would you be without it? – all this aroused feelings in Samson that no other woman had ever aroused. And thus, though he suspected her motives, she was the only woman who asked him the big, essential question of his life; the only one who knew the right question, and thus in effect asked him to hand over the keys to his secret, which other women were uninterested in, or perhaps feared. And therefore, amid the tempest of confused and conflicted feelings that her actions stirred in him, it's conceivable that a small hope was aroused too, that Delilah would be the one who would succeed in wresting some sort of 'answer' from him, a solution to the riddle that was entrenched deep inside him and that even he had not managed fully to understand.

Maybe somewhere deep in his soul, beneath the mountains of muscle, a voice told him that that it would be Delilah's persistence that would succeed in salvaging the buried self that had never managed to be redeemed in any other way; the self that very much wants to be revealed, to give of itself, to remove all that blocks and separates it from the rest of the world; to cast off the burden of mystery and riddle and accursed alienation; and to be at last 'like an ordinary man' – and, if so, might Samson also become intelligible to Samson himself?

For we have already recognised that an aura of discomfort always hovers around Samson, the enigma of the incompatibility and discord between his blessed divine mission and his earthy, material, corporeal (and often childlike) character and personality. Sometimes it is clear to the reader that Samson doesn't know himself at all, doesn't understand the role he fills in his own life story. But it is also possible – and this is truly a disturbing thought – that

God, *from the outset*, had no interest in Samson's being conscious of who he really was under the mantle of his mission, and what part he plays in the story, and what instrument he is in God's hands (and it suddenly seems that the 'use' to which God puts him – *shimush* in Hebrew – is the hidden meaning of Samson's name, *Shimshon*).

In which case, Samson is revealed here in all his misery. A lonely man, forever tortured, enslaved by a God who has chosen him for a demanding mission – the salvation of Israel – a task for which his personality and character are too weak; a man who manages time and again to become entangled in personal feuds with the enemies of Israel, thus endangering, failing, and disappointing his people, as well as the God who sent him.

And then it seems that Samson's entire physical essence is no more than a huge set of muscles that metamorphosed into great iron doors, 'city gates' designed to protect a fragile, vulnerable, interior human kernel; or, in fact, intended to prevent that kernel, which was in such dire need of redemption and self-revelation, from cracking open and finally becoming 'like an ordinary man'.

How can a man be redeemed? What is the natural, most desirable way for a man to open slightly the oppressive doors that wall him in, and allow that vulnerable kernel to reveal itself, to give and perhaps also be received?

'He fell in *love* with a woman.'

And perhaps into that one word is compressed Samson's small, bold, human, and bootless rebellion against the cruel use that the Lord has made of him. For as we know, in order for Samson to carry out his mission and strike the Philistines, God does not need for him to actually love a Philistine woman. To do his job all he needs is a prostitute, or a woman who is the 'right one' for him.

But if, however, the bond with Delilah did arouse in Samson something totally new, and was not designed merely to satisfy his compulsive need to be betrayed, to experience intimacy that is violated by strangers who turn it to their own purposes, then here, for the first time in his life, Samson fulfils his independent will by exercising the highest freedom available to him as a human being – and not as a tool in the hands of God – namely, emotional freedom, the freedom to love.

And if, on his part, this was true love, it may be surmised (perhaps only wishfully) that Samson allows Delilah to deceive him again and again because *he is hoping against hope that he is mistaken*; hoping that the next time he opens his eyes he will find himself in the room alone with his loved one, and the ambusher will be gone. The ambusher, whom Samson does not have to see in order to feel his eternal presence.

But then, after she says to him for the third time, 'Samson, the Philistines are upon you,' he understands, without a doubt or the chance of self-deception, that there is no love here. That the woman he loves, the only one he has ever loved, will not give him what he needs more than anything. That the fate imposed on him from the womb will forever pursue him, even into places of the greatest intimacy, and worst of all – that there is no way he can rebel against this fate, and therefore, it appears, he will not have another love in his life.

And probably because of this, more than for any other reason, 'he was wearied to death'.

And in simple words that he has been waiting all his life to utter, he reveals his secret to Delilah. And not only his secret, but *kol libo*, 'his whole heart', everything. Three times in two verses we find this phrase. And what is *kol libo*? 'No razor has ever touched my head, for I have been a Nazirite to God since I was in my mother's womb. If my hair were cut, my strength would leave me and I should become as weak as an ordinary man.' There, he has told her everything.

And when we hear the secret from his lips, and discover that this secret was *kol libo* – his heart of hearts – the thought arises that maybe it wasn't just the content of the secret that had been so important to Samson, but maybe the very fact that he had one. Thus it was vital to Samson not merely as a 'military secret', so to speak, but because it belonged to him alone, and no one else (except his mother) knew about it; it was his most private property, which had not been stained by strangers or by the excessive 'publicity' of his life.

Delilah senses at once that this time he is not deceiving her. There is the ring of truth here, and she summons the Philistine leaders and informs them that she has gotten to the bottom of the secret. They too can tell from her voice that this is really it. Again they come up to her room, and now bring the bundle of cash they have promised her.

This, of course, is a moment of trial for Delilah too: when the Philistine leaders told her, 'Coax him and find out what makes him so strong', she no doubt heard the challenge to her female powers of attraction ('See how strong *you* are', in effect.) But now, the extent that Samson had been able to resist her charms has cast doubt upon her seductive skills, and it's possible that she herself – maybe for the very first time – has begun to doubt her worth as a woman. The Philistine officers had surely begun to wonder about the long delay; and maybe even the ambusher in the room, who had repeatedly been a witness to Delilah's disappointments, had registered his impatience with a glance. It's therefore not hard to imagine that the erotic game between Samson and Delilah became more and more charged and tense for her too, and as her failures increased, so too did her personal stake.

And so, if in her first two tries she speaks to Samson the deceiver with incredible restraint – and we can almost see her teeth clenched in anger and resolution as she declares, 'You deceived me, you lied to me' – after her third failure she erupts, in a deep and womanly growl: 'How can you say you love me, when you don't confide in me?' She flings her rage and humiliation in his face, but also – maybe unwittingly – words that capture the very essence of his estrangement, and not only from her: *Ve-libcha ein iti*, as the Hebrew has it, you don't confide in me, 'your heart is not with me . . .'

And maybe these were the words she repeated to Samson, constantly pecking at his elemental wound,

the wound of his strangeness, and the words rever-
berated in the gaping void between his heart and
those he loved; and maybe this was the 'pestering'
that ultimately 'wearied him to death'.

Perhaps this is how it was. And because of this –
and for no other reason – he has confided *kol libo*,
nothing less than the whole heart that she had
accused of estrangement and deception; everything
that he had concealed and suppressed and hoarded
inside for so many years. In one momentary lapse he
gave it all to her, with that same sort of mad, breath-
less profligacy that sometimes afflicts the most
diehard of misers; with the foolish innocence of one
who believes that if he were to confide everything
to another person, all at once, in a kind of instant
transfusion, he would finally achieve a feeling of
genuine intimacy.

*       *       *

When the Philistine lords arrive, Samson is sleeping.
'She lulled him to sleep on her lap', says the Bible,

and we have already remarked that a moment before Delilah removed his locks Samson became like a child. It is as if he is returning to his origins, foetally curled on his 'mother's' lap.

Samson's eyes are closed, but under his eyelids there may well be a parade of memories and images: a long, tempestuous, arduous journey, with Samson marching, step after step, to the place it all began, where it all became twisted together – mother, child, betrayal.

And here may be found something of an answer to the question we posed earlier – why would Samson want to re-enact, again and again, precisely the most damaging feeling he had ever experienced, which had poisoned his life from the start? Or in other words, why do human beings compulsively repeat destructive experiences, re-creating in the course of their lives the dysfunctional relationships and the self-defeating situations that arouse their worst, most toxic feelings?

Is this not – among other reasons – because it is precisely there, at the epicentre of humiliation and alienation and misunderstanding, that a person feels the most 'himself' as he 'really is', in other words, as he was at the origin of his life, at the very beginning? He may have been hugged, swaddled in love and warmth, rocked gently to sleep on lap or breast, but it was there too that he was branded – if not out of malice – and scarred, imprinted with the consciousness of existential strangeness, the bitter feeling of being accidental or alien, even, in a sense, within his own private, intimate biography.

There, in that place, Samson's mother uttered the terrible words, 'until his dying day', or some other devastating remark that parents make, sometimes off-handedly, about their child. There they sealed his fate, for his whole life, and it is for this very reason, it seems, that he is compelled to go back there, because that is where the grim foundational drama of his existence takes place. There, in a strange way, he most feels the fire of being of alive, even as it burns him again and again. There too, within us all, sadly flickers the eternal flame of self-recognition as men and women who are, in the end, separated and isolated from one another, mysterious and even 'unknowable' to others – even perhaps to ourselves – and therefore, also, endlessly lonely.

Samson is asleep, exhausted. Possibly he is filled with unexpected relief after giving away his secret, and no longer needing to steel all his muscles to defend it. His journey is over. Now he can be like other men. 'My strength would leave me', he has explained, as we recall, just a moment earlier to Delilah, 'and I should become as weak as an ordinary man', *kechol ha-adam*.

'As *every* other man', he literally said. But earlier, when Delilah had bound him, he said to her – twice – that he would weaken *ke'achad ha'adam*, like *any* other man, the word *achad* meaning 'one', as if still wanting, unconsciously, to retain his individuality. Now he forfeits this too, and reveals to her how he can become like every man, tasting these words for the first time.

But maybe it is not a weakness, an illness, to be like everyone else. Maybe this is what Samson, in his heart of hearts, has wanted his whole life. And so too, in Lea Goldberg's poem 'Samson's Love':

> '. . . *And perhaps even he didn't know*
> *Of his prophet and Nazirite's test,*
> *How the simplest riddle of all*
> *Was the breakable heart in his breast.*'[28]

★   ★   ★

Delilah summons 'a man' – apparently the one who had waited in ambush in the room – but it is she herself, and not the man, who cuts off the seven locks of the sleeping Samson's hair. Maybe she does it in order to spare him a bit of the humiliation of being shorn by strangers. Or maybe this way she is in fact humiliating him all the more. And maybe this is her way of saying goodbye and thus to experience again, distilled into a single action, the strong feelings that flowed between them. Thousands of years later, it is possible to imagine her shifting expression as she performs the deed, with an erotic touch on one hand

and overtones of castration on the other, and perhaps the thin smile of a woman whose charms have not failed her.

His strength has already slipped away, but he is still asleep and unaware of this. She begins to taunt him. She cries out again, for the fourth time, 'Samson, the Philistines are upon you!' He awakes and says to himself, 'I will break loose and shake myself free as I did the other times.' He flexes his muscles as he had done previously, and then discovers that 'the Lord had departed from him'.

The Philistines in the room immediately gouge out his eyes. The eyes that had been so alert, impassioned, hungry, restless. 'Samson followed his eyes', commented the rabbis of the Talmud, 'which is why the Philistines gouged them out.'[29] Just as he uprooted the gates of Gaza, now they pull out the gates of his face and soul. Who can begin to imagine what Samson is going through? One can only assume that it is not only the physical agony of the gouging that consumes him, not only the rage and pain over his lover's betrayal. Samson is now prey to a sensation he has not known since the day he was first moved as a youth by the spirit of God: his enormous strength is gone. His body does not respond as before. Now it too is foreign to him. His body has also betrayed him.

\*   \*   \*

His eyes plucked out, bound with bronze chains, Samson is taken by the Philistines to Gaza, where he is put to work as a mill-slave in the prison. Now, trudging endlessly around the grindstone, he spends his days looking inward, perhaps beginning to see what he could not see before he became blind: the whole spectacle of his life, the manipulative destiny that denied him free choice or the right to protest, or a single minute of tranquillity.

Circling and grinding, stripped of his special secret, his crown of Nazirite glory, and of any superhuman strength greater than that of his muscles alone. In the sunset of his life he learns the limits of his power and maybe also his own true essence, freed at last from the gusts of the great, tyrannical bellows known as the 'spirit of the Lord'. Quite likely he can, now and then, even revel in a simple sense of self, of being someone tolerable and altogether human, someone that was stolen even before he was born.

(And it may have been a bit of a relief, when Delilah removed the weight of those seven long locks of hair that had never been cut, that cascaded down his face and surrounded his body and which undoubtedly had further detached him from the world at large.)

Thus pass his days. His hair is starting to grow back and with it his strength. According to the narrative, Samson is deep into his work at the grind-stone. And yet it may well be that the grinding had another aspect entirely: the verb 'to grind' in Hebrew carries a clear sexual connotation, which may be found as early as the Book of Job – 'May my wife grind for another, and may others kneel over her'[30] – and continues into vulgar Israeli slang. Perhaps this was the origin of the legends that cropped up over the years about how Samson spent his last days: the Talmud tells how 'everyone brought his wife to him to the prison that she might bear a child by him'.[31] This suggestion, titillating at first, quickly translates into another means of abusing and humiliating Samson by turning him into a stud bull. What we have here, in the end, is a cruel and grotesque extension of the great curse of his life, the curse of strangeness.

One day they take him out of the prison and bring him before a jubilant crowd. The Philistine nobles gather to offer a great sacrifice to their gods and to rejoice that Dagon has delivered Samson into their hands. Samson stands before them. They look at him with amazement. Apparently even in defeat he gives the impression of being a wonder of nature, eliciting all the more kudos to Dagon for having triumphed over him.

After they have feasted their eyes on him, he is returned to jail and the Philistines continue their celebration. And then, well into their cups, they demand that Samson return and 'dance for us'. They bring him back from the prison. 'And he danced for them.' Here too, there are those who interpret this as some sort of 'sex show', as the Hebrew verb here, *letzahek*, is used now and again in the Bible to describe a sexual act.[32] In any event, Samson is certainly humiliated and ridiculed in full view of the merry-making Philistines.

He hears the carousing Philistines but cannot see a thing. He is the only Israelite amid three thousand Philistines, men and women, 'watching Samson dance'. One boy stands beside him, holding him by the hand and leading him. Samson, the inveterate warrior, immediately senses an opportunity. He asks the boy to place his hands on the pillars. 'Let me feel the pillars,' he says, using a rare locution, *hamisheni*, that implies a warm caress – in chilling contrast to what Samson is about to do. The boy places his hands upon the pillars. Samson's fingers now make their final contact with the world, disconnecting from the actual, tactile sensation and recollecting instead everything they had they previously touched, men and women, lion and foxes, honey and ropes and rock, the jawbone of an ass, cool spring water and a prostitute and the gates of a city, and Delilah.

'O Lord God,' cries Samson bitterly, 'please remember me, and give me strength just this once, O God, to take revenge on the Philistines, if only for one of my two eyes.' It is the shattering cry of one who knows that his God has abandoned him, and who has come to realise that he has failed abjectly in performing the mission for which he was created. Samson in this hour addresses God with three different, holy Hebrew names, as if he is trying to enter the heart of God through all of its gates, to reach a place where a portal will be opened into a most personal, intimate deity, the one who chose him and took him when he was still in the womb, the one whose spirit had empowered Samson all his life. He does not know, of course, whether God will answer his prayers this time, as He did in the Rock of Etam, when Samson nearly died of thirst. Indeed a much fresher memory is the moment he said to himself, 'I will break loose and shake myself free as I did the other times', only to discover to his dismay that Delilah had shorn his hair and depleted his power, and that his God had left him.

With a mixture of uncertainty, desperation, and hope he grabs hold of the pillars with all his strength, embracing one with his right arm and the other with his left, 'the two middle pillars that the temple rested upon'. What runs through his mind now, as he is about to die? Is it possible that the contact with the two pillars conjures the memory of his parents, his father and mother, and with it his longstanding, incessant pain over never really having parents at all? Maybe he is also pierced by the recognition that there was always a pair between whom he stood, yearning to embrace them, two and only two, without any foreign presence: the pillars of this temple, two foxes with a burning torch, the gateposts of Gaza.

He brings about his own death, as the Hebrew has it, in a *bayit*, a house, a home. He, who from birth, indeed from the womb, was exiled in effect

from any kind of home; whose entire private life
had been hijacked; who never had a home of his
own and never really belonged either to his own
people or to the people into whose midst his urges
had propelled him. He, who slept with many women
but had no child of his own; he, whose umbilical
cord had been severed, as it were, at both ends, now
stands in the middle of a house that 'rests upon' –
*nachon* in Hebrew – two pillars. But *nachon* also
means 'proper': at last – how ironic – *bayit nachon*,
a proper home.

'O Lord God,' cries the blind Samson, 'please
remember me, and give me strength just this
once . . .' He pulls the pillars with all his strength
and only then, as they begin to crack and move,
does he learn that his God has not abandoned him
after all. He crashes the house down upon the
Philistine lords and all the other people within.
'Those who were slain by him as he died', it is written, 'outnumbered those who had been slain by him
when he lived', and in the echo chamber of our own
time and place there is no escaping the thought that

Samson was, in a sense, the first suicide-killer; and although the circumstances of his deed were different from those familiar to us from the daily reality of the streets of Israel, it may be that the act itself established in human consciousness a mode of murder and revenge directed at innocent victims, which has been perfected in recent years. [33]

And only after his death is he truly brought home. 'His brothers and all his father's household came down and carried him up and buried him in the tomb of his father Manoah, between Zorah and Eshtaol.' There is no way of knowing whether these were actual 'brothers' who were later born to the same parents, or other relatives, or simply members of his tribe. But it would appear that his whole extended family gathers around him now, only now. With pity and concern they come down and carry him up and bury him in a place where, at last, he will find perfect peace.

Samson is gone. For a moment all is silence, and then the thought arises that the rabbis of old were on the mark when they connected the word *lefa'amo* –

referring to Samson's miraculous empowerment – with the image of a ringing bell, *pa'amon*, declaring that 'the divine spirit', the *Shekhinah*, 'kept ringing in front of him like a bell'.[34] For it is as if a bell has suddenly fallen silent, a bell that began ringing from the moment the spirit began to arouse Samson. All his life Samson seemed like a giant bell in the hands of a celestial providence that would strike and tinkle it at will, with a strange mix of tones that some-times sounded like music but more often a grating, violent cacophony. An unfortunate bell, swung back and forth with unrelenting force, whose tintinnab-ulations echoed from the towns of the tribe of Dan to the cities of the Philistines.

But before he perished, at the precise moment that he was engraved in memory, myth, and art, Samson embraced the two supporting pillars and brought them down, the columns, the house, the Philistines, himself. And for one last instant – as in all of Samson's astonishing exploits – the whole thing boils down to one sharp, penetrating statement: Let my soul die as it had always lived. Without being truly close to another soul, alone, among foreigners who sought without surcease to injure it, ridicule it, betray it. Let my soul die with the Philistines.

# Notes

1 The Bible, of course, presents the story of
Samson as a 'drama of fate', and less as a 'drama
of character'. Nonetheless, the way the story's
actors, Samson in particular, are drawn cannot
help but lead the contemporary reader – armed
with the qualities and sensibilities of our own
time – to the collision and interaction of 'fate'
and 'personality'. Moreover, as the story devel-
ops, it turns out that it may, in fact, be Samson's
personality that prevents him from realising the
destiny for which he is meant.

2 Vladimir (Ze'ev) Jabotinsky (1880–1940) was a
Russian-born Zionist leader whose novel *Samson
the Nazarite* was serialised in the Russian Zionist
journal *Razsvet* in 1926, published in book form
in 1927, and translated into English in 1930. It
served as the basis for Cecil B. DeMille's 1949
film *Samson and Delilah*.

3 Babylonian Talmud (BT), Tractate Berachot 61a.

4 Professor Yair Zakovitch of the Hebrew
University, in his book *The Life of Samson*, points
out that Manoah here calls his wife 'the woman',
implying alienation, stemming perhaps from
suspicion; and that Adam, who becomes
estranged from his wife Eve after she seduces
him into eating the fruit of the Tree of
Knowledge, says to God: 'The woman You put at
my side – she gave me of the tree, and I ate.'
Zakovitch, *Hayei Shimshon* ('The Life of Samson'
[Hebrew: Jerusalem, 1982]), p. 49. In this
connection, let us note that the Jewish-Roman
historian Josephus Flavius, in his monumental
work *Jewish Antiquities* (V:276), asserts that
Manoah was 'madly enamoured of his wife and
hence inordinately jealous'. Translated by H. St.
J. Thackeray and Ralph Marcus (Cambridge and
London, 1958), Vol. V, p. 125.

5 Zakovitch (p. 70) points out that the biblical
text does not provide the derivation of Samson's
name, a rarity among major biblical figures. He

contends that the biblical narrator wished to
avoid any association of Samson and the sun, a
linkage with strong pagan connotations.

[6] BT Sotah 10a.

[7] Josephus Flavius, *Jewish Antiquities* V:285. Trans.
Thackeray and Marcus, Vol. V, p. 129.

[8] BT Sotah 10a.

[9] Jerusalem Talmud, Sotah 7b.

[10] Zohar I:194a.

[11] One finds in Jewish sources an ambivalence
toward the phenomenon of the Nazirite. There
are those who saw it as a state of great spiritual
elevation, which not everyone is capable of
achieving. Thus, the prophet Amos: 'And I raised
up prophets from among your sons and Nazirites
from among your young men' (Amos 2:11); and
in the Talmud, Rabbi Eleazer. But there were also
those who regarded extreme asceticism and isolation as sinful – for example, the rabbis Eleazar
HaKappar and Samuel (see BT Ta'anit 11a.).

[12] I Samuel 13:19.

[13] It is interesting to mention, in this context, the

hypothesis of the archaeologist Yigael Yadin, who raised the possibility that the tribe of Dan was closely related to the sea people known as the Danai, so much so as to complicate Dan's inclusion as one of the tribes of Israel. See Isaac Avishur, 'Dan', *Encyclopaedia Judaica* 5: 1255–9; also Yigael Yadin, 'And Dan, why did he remain in ships?', *Australian Journal of Biblical Archaeology*, 1 (1968): 9–23.

14 Genesis 49:16, 18.

15 I Kings 10:27.

16 In his commentary on the Book of Judges, the nineteenth-century rabbinical scholar Malbim wrote that 'apparently this was the time of the grape harvest, and as they reached the path through the vineyards Samson changed course, in accordance with [the ancient dictum] "Go around, we say to a Nazirite, do not go near a vineyard."'

17 Bees, of course, have a highly developed sense of smell, and thus it is unlikely that they would settle in a rotting carcass, but would do

so only later, after the stench had dissipated
and only a skeleton remained. This observation
supports the conjecture that a year had passed
between Samson's battle with the lion and his
return to Timnah. See Haim Shmueli, *Hidat
Shimshon* ('Samson's Riddle' [Hebrew: Tel Aviv,
1964]), p. 58.

[18] The Anglo-Jewish writer Linda Grant, in an
article entitled 'Jews behaving badly', connects
Samson with the Golem of Prague. The Golem,
according to Jewish legend, was created by
Rabbi Judah Loew of Prague, known as the
Maharal, in the sixteenth century. The Maharal
fashioned the Golem out of clay in order to
fight off the enemies of the Jews. When the
Maharal would shove into the creature's mouth
a slip of paper on which was written the inef-
fable name of God, the Golem would come to
life and do the rabbi's bidding. In keeping with
this parallelism, one can read the paper with
God's name on it as a concrete expression of the
'spirit of the Lord' that animated Samson. See

Linda Grant, 'Jews behaving badly: Samson, Sharon, and other "tough Jews"', *Jewish Quarterly* 49, 2 (Summer 2002): 48–52.

[19] Genesis 2:24.

[20] The idea of Samson's compulsive need to be betrayed by women was raised and explored in depth by the Israeli psychiatrist Ilan Kutz in his article, 'Samson's complex', in which he analyses the 'behavioural disturbance' – as he put it – of the biblical Samson. According to Kutz, the essence of this disturbance is 'the compulsion to re-enact the experience of betrayal by women, followed by destructive acts of rage against others, and ultimately against their own tormented selves'. Kutz emphasises the problematic behaviour of the mother as the source of Samson's psychological disorder: 'Whether or not this nameless stranger is accepted as a messenger of God, it is possible to infer that there were rumours and whispers surrounding the circumstances of Samson's birth. Perhaps . . . Samson's childhood

was enveloped by a deep sense of shame,
related to his mother's questionable behaviour
or his father's uncertain paternity.' Ilan Kutz,
'Samson's complex: The compulsion to re-enact
betrayal and rage', *British Journal of Medical
Psychology*, 62 (1989): 123–34.

[21] Rainer Maria Rilke, *Letters to a Young Poet*,
translated by Stephen Mitchell (New York,
1986), p. 40.

[22] See II Chronicles 11:6.

[23] Though there is, in Gaza City itself, a hill
known to this day as 'Samson's Grave'.

[24] A comprehensive survey of the representations
of Samson in world art and culture may be
found in David Fishelov, *Mahlafot Shimshon*
('Samson's Locks' [Hebrew: Jerusalem, 2000]).

[25] See Kutz, 'Samson's complex', n. 20.

[26] Ilan Kutz, focusing on Samson's death-wish,
interprets this scene as an unspoken suicide pact:
'Both Samson and Delila [sic] take part in this
death dance. If Delila is leading Samson
consciously on the deadly floor of betrayal,

Samson is unconsciously manipulating Delila in the dance of his suicide. It may even be surmised that Samson meticulously and repeatedly auditioned his female partner before giving her the role of the loving-betraying executioner, and that the three early betrayals by Delila were but trial runs before she could be entrusted with the real thing.' (Kutz, 'Samson's complex', p. 130.)

[27] BT Sotah 9b.

[28] Lea Goldberg, 'Samson's love', in the collection *Barak Ba-Boker* ('Lightning in the Morning' [Hebrew: Merhavia, Israel, 1957]), p. 112. Goldberg (1911–1970) was an important Hebrew modernist poet.

[29] BT Sotah 9b.

[30] Job 31:10.

[31] BT Sotah 10a.

[32] For one example, we have Potiphar's wife accusing Joseph: 'She called out to her servants and said to them, "Look, he had to bring us a Hebrew to dally with us!"' – *letzahek banu*. 'This one came to lie with me . . .' (Genesis 39:14).

[33] Rabbi Saadiah Gaon, the tenth-century leader of Babylonian Jewry, commented in his *Book of Beliefs and Opinions* on the damaging effect of the lust for revenge upon the soul of the avenger as well as his victims. Saadiah brings Samson's final act as an example of an especially extreme and destructive case of revenge. In other rabbinic literature, we generally find no condemnation of Samson's final revenge, although his aggressive behaviour is sometimes censured. Saadiah Gaon, *The Book of Beliefs and Opinions*, Treatise 10, Chapter 13. Translated by Samuel Rosenblatt (New Haven, 1948), pp. 390–2.

[34] BT Sotah 9b.

Born in Jerusalem in 1954, DAVID GROSSMAN is the leading Israeli writer of his generation and his work has been translated into twenty-five languages. He is the author of six internationally acclaimed novels, and two powerful journalistic accounts, as well as a number of children's books and a play. Grossman has been presented with numerous awards, including Chevalier of the Order of Arts and Letters (France). He lives with his wife and children in a suburb of Jerusalem.